THE
MONEY
RESOURCE
GUIDE

Grants, Business Capital & Smart Money
Strategies for Sustainable Growth

FOURTH EDITION

RENEE BOBB

**The Money Resource Guide: Grants, Business Capital &
Smart Money Strategies for Sustainable Growth**

Fourth Edition

Empowerment Training & Development Coaching Firm

Renee Bobb, Empowerment Coach
(615) 753-5647
bobbrenee@yahoo.com
https://reneebobbtraining.com/
https://stan.store/reneebobbtraining
https://www.skool.com/thegrantfundingacademy

ISBN: 979-8-218-65712-3

Library of Congress Cataloging-in-Publication Data
Printed in the United States of America

In this resource guide you will find:

- **A step-by-step roadmap to launch and grow your grant funding journey**—including how to get "Grant Ready" and uncover hidden opportunities most business owners overlook.

- **Insider strategies to master the grant application process**—from assembling your dream team to understanding what funders truly want and how to pitch like a pro.

- **Cutting-edge AI tools and automation techniques**—learn how to use ChatGPT, prompt engineering, and data to streamline your research, writing, and compliance.

- **Diverse funding strategies beyond grants**—including crowdfunding, corporate sponsorships, pitch competitions, and business plan contests to multiply your funding sources.

- **A curated list of over 200 grant funding opportunities**—organized by business type, industry, and mission (including women, minority, veteran-owned, tech, healthcare, arts, and more).

DISCLAIMER

The Publisher and the Author make no representations or warranties with respect to the accuracy or completeness of the contents of this work and specifically disclaim all warranties, including without limitation warranties of career empowerment for a particular purpose. No warranty may be created or extended by sales or promotional materials. The advise and strategies contained herein may not be suitable for every situation. This work is sold with the understanding that the Publisher is not engaged in rendering legal, accounting, or other professional services. If professional assistance is required, the services of a competent professional person should be sought. Neither the Publisher nor the Author shall be liable for damages arising here from. The fact that an organization or website is referred to in this work as a citation and /or a potential source of further information does not mean that the Author or the Publisher endorses the information the organization or website may provide or recommendations it may make. Further, readers should be aware that internet websites listed in this work may have changed or disappeared between when this work was written and when it is read.

DEDICATION

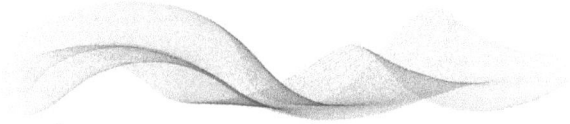

In loving memory of my amazing mom,
Aretia Bobb-Pate.
Your love, strength, and unwavering friendship live on in my heart.
Thank you for believing in me and inspiring
everything I do. I love you always.

This book is also lovingly dedicated to my daughter, Keyana, and my
son, Keymani. May you grow up knowing the power of ownership, the
value of purpose, and the courage to turn your dreams into reality.
You are my greatest motivation.

ACKNOWLEDGEMENT

I want to take a moment to extend my deepest gratitude to everyone who has supported me on this journey—personally, professionally, and spiritually.

To my family and close friends, thank you for your unwavering encouragement, patience, and love. Your belief in me has been the fuel behind every page of this guide.

To my amazing clients, students, and community—you are the reason this work matters. Your commitment to growth, your boldness in chasing funding, and your willingness to do the work continue to inspire me every single day.

To my team—thank you for your dedication, creativity, and support in helping bring this guide to life. This wouldn't be possible without you.

And to every reader holding this book right now: thank you for trusting me to walk alongside you in your grant funding and financial empowerment journey. I don't take it lightly, and I am honored to be part of your path.

To your continued growth and prosperity,
– Renee Bobb

CONTENTS

Introduction   xv

CHAPTER 1: UNDERSTANDING GRANT FUNDING   1

- Launching Your Grant Funding Journey   3
- Myths About Securing Grant Funding   7
- What is a Grant?   13
- Where Do Grants Come From?   15
- How Do You Get Grant Ready?   20

CHAPTER 2: MASTERING THE GRANT APPLICATION PROCESS   25

- Building Your Professional Team   27
- How to Find a Professional Grant Writer?   35
- Finding Hot Grant Opportunities   39
- The Psychology of Funders: Understanding What
  Grantors Want   43
- How to Pitch Your Business or Nonprofit for
  Grant Funding   45
- The Secret to Grant Writing Success   50

CHAPTER 3: AI & TECHNOLOGY IN GRANT FUNDING

CHAPTER 3: AI & TECHNOLOGY IN GRANT FUNDING   **55**

- AI Tools for Finding and Writing Grants   57
- How AI is Changing the Grant Funding Landscape   58
- Leveraging Data & Automation for Smarter Grant Applications   59
- Using AI for Grant Research, Proposal Writing & Compliance   60
- Introduction to ChatGPT   61
- AI Tools to Find Opportunities   63
- How to Use Prompt Engineering Effectively   64
- Sample Prompt You Can Try   67

CHAPTER 4: DIVERSE FUNDING STRATEGIES FOR BUSINESS OWNERS & NONPROFITS   **71**

- Diverse Funding Strategies for Business Owners & Nonprofits   73
- Top 12 Options to Finance Your Dream   77
- How to Find and Win RFP (Request for Proposal) Opportunities   80
- Crowdfunding Resources   84
- Corporate Sponsorships: How to Secure Business Partnerships   87
- Business Plan Competitions: A Hidden Gem for Funding and Exposure   91
- Pitch Competitions: Ace Your Next Opportunity   94

CHAPTER 5: GRANT FUNDING OPPORTUNITIES & RESOURCES   **99**

- Grants for Women-Owned Businesses   101
- Grants for Minority Entrepreneurs   108
- Grants for Startups & Small Businesses   113
- Grants for Nonprofits & Community-Based Organizations   118

- Grants for Veteran-Owned Businesses   123
- Grants for Healthcare & Wellness Initiatives   127
- Grants for Arts & Creative Enterprises   130
- Grants for Sustainability & Green Businesses   136
- Grants for Technology & Innovation   138
- International Grants for Businesses and Nonprofits   141

In Conclusion   149

Tracking Form   153

About Business Coach Renee Bobb   165

INTRODUCTION

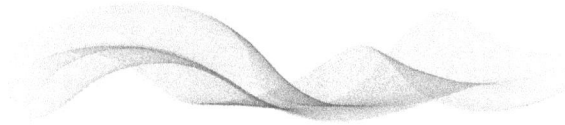

You are holding the ultimate resource for unlocking the funding your business or nonprofit needs to grow, thrive, and create lasting impact. *The Money Resource Guide: Grants, Business Capital & Smart Money Strategies for Sustainable Growth (Fourth Edition)* was designed with you in mind, the visionary, the builder, the change-maker who's ready to take bold action and fund your next big move.

Inside, you'll find proven strategies, expert insights, AI-powered tools, and hundreds of real grant opportunities. Whether you're just starting your funding journey or looking to scale to the next level, this guide will give you the clarity, confidence, and step-by-step direction to secure the money you need to fuel your mission.

This is more than a book. It's a blueprint. And now it's in your hands.

Let's get funded.

CHAPTER 1
UNDERSTANDING GRANT FUNDING

LAUNCHING YOUR GRANT FUNDING JOURNEY

Many people dream of securing grant funding but often find themselves overwhelmed by the process. The biggest challenge isn't just finding the right grants, it's knowing where to start. If you're reading this book, chances are you've wondered how other businesses and nonprofits seem to effortlessly secure funding while you struggle to even get a response. The truth is, there's a system to winning grant money, and once you understand it, everything changes.

I didn't always know how to navigate the grant funding world. Like many entrepreneurs, I started out by chasing every opportunity I could find, hoping one of them would work. But I quickly realized that applying for grants without a plan was like throwing darts in the dark. I needed a strategy, one that would allow me to consistently secure funding, not just for myself, but for the thousands of business owners and nonprofit leaders I would go on to help.

Over the past twenty years, I've trained more than 100,000 business owners and nonprofit agencies on how to find, apply for, and win grant funding. I've worked with entrepreneurs who had no idea where to begin and guided them to securing multi-year grants that changed the course of their businesses. I've taught organizations how to diversify their revenue so they weren't relying solely on one source of funding. I've even helped my clients win over $2.3 million in grants and pitch competitions, giving them the financial stability they needed to grow.

One of the biggest game changers in my work has been the integration of AI into the grant writing process. Early on, I saw how difficult and time-consuming research could be, and I knew there had to be a better way. That's when I started teaching business owners how to use AI tools to streamline their funding journey. I showed them how to automate research, track grant deadlines, and even build AI-powered bots to assist them with writing applications. What once took weeks could now be done in days, and for some, even hours.

Recognizing the need for a dedicated space where business owners and nonprofits could get continuous support, I created the Grant Funding Academy Community on Skool. (https://www.skool.com/thegrantfundingacademy) It's a space where entrepreneurs can connect, share opportunities, and receive hands-on guidance in securing funding. In this community, I teach people how to position their businesses for grants, leverage AI for efficiency, and tap into alternative funding streams beyond traditional grants.

When I first started applying for grants, I knew I needed to be strategic. I didn't just apply to random opportunities; I focused on building partnerships with organizations that had access to funding. One of the smartest moves I made was working with the Women's Business Center and the Small Business Administration. At the time, they had a major grant focused on helping women who were transitioning out of prison. Instead of trying to apply for the grant myself, I aligned my business with their mission. By doing so, I was able to get my services funded and bring my business into the Tennessee Prison for Women, where I provided training sessions and sold my books in bulk.

That was a defining moment for me. I realized that winning grants wasn't just about applying, it was about becoming the solution that funding organizations were looking to invest in.

Later, I had another eye-opening experience when I applied for the American Express Top 100 Black Women Entrepreneurs Grant. Unlike traditional grants that required pages of documentation, this application was short and simple. They wanted to know who I was, what my business did, and how the pandemic had impacted me. It took me less than 90 minutes to complete, and I submitted it without overthinking the process.

Weeks later, I received an email telling me that I had been selected as one of the winners. Just like that, $25,000 was deposited into my business account. It was a reminder that sometimes, the biggest opportunities don't require long, complicated applications, they just require you to take action.

I've seen so many business owners hesitate to apply for grants because they assume the process will be too difficult or they think they won't qualify. But the reality is, there are grants out there for nearly every type of business. I've won grants for my own ventures, including the Hilton Hotel Grant, which was unique because instead of receiving a check or direct deposit, I was given a pre-loaded credit card to use for business expenses.

The more I learned about securing funding, the more I realized that grants are just one piece of the puzzle. I started looking into other ways to raise capital and discovered the power of crowdfunding. When I purchased my women's professional basketball team, I knew I didn't want to use my own money to fund the operation. Instead, I launched a crowdfunding campaign on IFundWomen (https://www.ifundwomen.com) At the time, I wasn't sure what to expect, but I ended up raising over 360% of my original goal.

What made IFundWomen so powerful was their partnerships with major corporations. As the platform grew, companies began reaching out, wanting to provide funding to women entrepreneurs. That meant that not only did I raise money through my campaign, but I also became eligible for additional grants that were being distributed directly through the platform. It was another lesson in positioning, when you align yourself with the right opportunities, funding starts coming to you.

These experiences shaped my approach to teaching grant funding. I no longer believe in chasing opportunities aimlessly. Instead, I believe in building a strategy that allows funding to come to you. That's exactly what I teach inside the Grant Funding Academy Community, and it's what I will guide you through in this book.

Securing grant funding isn't about luck, it's about having the right tools, the right knowledge, and the right strategy. Throughout these pages, I'll show you how to build your team, find the right grants, track your applications, and create a sustainable funding plan for your business or nonprofit.

By the time you finish this book, you won't just understand grant funding you'll know how to win it.

MYTHS ABOUT SECURING GRANT FUNDING

There are countless myths about grant funding, and unfortunately, these misconceptions hold many business owners and nonprofit leaders back. Some people assume the process is too complicated, while others believe grants are only for certain types of businesses. These myths create hesitation, causing many people to miss out on opportunities that could help them grow and scale.

Before diving into the details of how to secure funding, let's take a moment to clear up some of these common misunderstandings. The first step to winning grant funding is shifting your mindset. If you've been listening to people who say grant funding is impossible, I encourage you to stop. Instead, start having conversations with people who have successfully secured grant funding. Their stories will be different. They will share strategies, insights, and lessons that will help you see what's possible.

Now, let's break down some of the biggest myths about grant funding.

MYTH 1: YOU MUST PAY THE MONEY BACK

One of the most common misconceptions is that grants function like loans, that at some point, you'll be expected to repay the money. This is completely false. Grants are free money given by organizations that want to support businesses, nonprofits, and individuals who align with their mission. As long as you use the funding as outlined in your application, you do not have to pay it back.

MYTH 2: GRANTS ARE ONLY FOR MINORITY BUSINESS OWNERS

There is a widely held belief that only minority-owned businesses can qualify for grants. While there are grants dedicated to minority entrepreneurs, there are just as many opportunities open to all types of business owners, regardless of race, gender, or background. Grants exist for women, veterans, rural businesses, tech startups, creatives, healthcare providers, and more. The key is knowing where to look.

MYTH 3: YOU MUST BE A SEASONED BUSINESS OWNER TO WIN GRANT FUNDING

Many aspiring entrepreneurs assume they need to be in business for five or ten years before they can even think about applying for grants. This is far from true. Some grants do require businesses to be established for a certain number of years, but many specifically target startups and early-stage entrepreneurs.

If you are just starting out, don't count yourself out. Focus on finding grants that align with where you are in your business journey. If you have a strong vision and a clear plan, you can absolutely win funding, even if you're just getting started.

MYTH 4: YOU MUST PAY A FEE TO ACCESS THE BEST GRANTS

If someone is trying to charge you money to access a list of "exclusive" grants, be careful. Grant information is publicly available and can be found through government websites, corporate funding programs, and nonprofit organizations.

Getting access to a curated grant list can significantly reduce the time and energy you spend researching opportunities, allowing you to focus on preparing stronger applications. While hiring a grant writer or consultant to help craft a compelling proposal can be a smart investment, make sure any grant list you invest in provides real value, is regularly updated, and includes actionable opportunities tailored to your needs.

MYTH 5: YOU MUST BE POOR AND STRUGGLING TO GET A GRANT

Many people assume that grants are only given to businesses and nonprofits in financial crisis. While some grants do focus on helping struggling organizations, many are designed to support growth, expansion, and innovation. You don't have to be in a financial crisis to qualify, you just need to align with the funder's mission and present a strong application.

MYTH 6: IT TAKES HOURS AND HOURS TO APPLY FOR GRANT FUNDING

It's true that applying for grants can take time, but that doesn't mean it has to be a long and painful process. The key to speeding up the process is having a system in place.

One of the most effective ways to streamline grant applications is by using the Grant Funding Application Answer Key, which you'll find in the resource section of this book. This tool allows you to compile your most commonly needed answers, such as your business mission, financial details, impact statements, and funding needs, in one document. Since most grants ask similar questions, you can use this resource to quickly pull information without having to rewrite everything from scratch.

AI tools can also make the process faster and more efficient. Many business owners struggle with crafting clear, compelling responses, and that's where AI-powered writing assistants come in. Instead of spending hours struggling with wording, you can use AI to refine your answers, ensuring they are well-structured, professional, and in alignment with the grant's objectives.

By combining AI tools with a well-organized Answer Key, you'll cut down the application time significantly and be able to apply for more grants with ease.

MYTH 7: YOU SHOULD NOT BE USING AI TO WRITE YOUR GRANT APPLICATION

There is a growing misconception that AI should not be used when applying for grants. While it is true that you should never rely on AI to fully write your grant application, you should absolutely use it to enhance your answers. AI can help refine your responses, ensuring they are clear, concise, and professional. It can also assist in aligning your application with the funder's mission by highlighting key themes that strengthen your proposal. Additionally, AI improves grammar, clarity, and structure, making your application more compelling and easier to read.

However, your answers must come from you. Funders want to hear your voice, your passion, and your unique story. AI should be a tool to improve your responses, not a shortcut to avoid writing them yourself.

The key is to use AI strategically, to polish and enhance your application while still ensuring that it reflects your vision and purpose.

MYTH 8: YOU HAVE TO BE A NONPROFIT TO GET A GRANT

One of the biggest misconceptions about grant funding is that it's only available to nonprofits. While it's true that nonprofits often have more grant opportunities, there are thousands of grants available for for-profit businesses as well.

Many corporations, government agencies, and private foundations offer grants specifically for small businesses, startups, and industry-specific initiatives such as healthcare, sustainability, education, and technology. If you are a business owner, don't assume that grants are off-limits, there are opportunities out there for you, too.

In the Current Grant Opportunities & Resources section of this book, I've included an updated list of active grants that business owners, start-ups, and entrepreneurs may qualify for. Whether you're a woman-owned business, a veteran entrepreneur, a tech startup, or a creative professional, you'll find specific grant opportunities that align with your industry and business goals. Instead of assuming grants aren't for you, take the time to explore these funding options, you might be surprised at how many opportunities are available!

MYTH 9: WHEN YOU APPLY FOR A GRANT, YOU ARE GUARANTEED TO WIN

This is one of the most dangerous myths because it sets unrealistic expectations. Applying for a grant does not guarantee that you will win. Grant funding is competitive, and just like any other opportunity, success comes with persistence and strategy.

I once worked with a client who applied for her very first grant, and she won it. While that does happen, it is not the norm. Most people don't win their first grant. That's why I created "Funding Friday," a strategy where I commit to applying for three to five grants every single Friday. The more grants you apply for, the greater your chances of securing funding.

The key to winning grants is consistency. If you treat grant funding like a numbers game and continue applying, refining, and improving your applications, you will eventually win.

SHIFTING YOUR MINDSET FOR GRANT SUCCESS

If you've believed any of these myths, now is the time to let them go. Grant funding is not impossible, it just requires the right approach, the right tools, and the right mindset.

Throughout this book, you'll learn everything you need to know to find, apply for, and win grant funding. But the most important thing you can do right now is take action. The difference between those who win grants and those who don't isn't luck, it's persistence.

It's time to break free from these myths and start securing the funding you deserve.

WHAT IS A GRANT?

A grant is money awarded by the government, corporations, or private organizations for a specific purpose, and the best part is, it doesn't have to be paid back. However, there's no such thing as "something for nothing." When a funder provides grant money, they expect something in return, whether it's community impact, business growth, or alignment with their mission.

Grant funders typically provide detailed guidelines on how the money can be used. Some grants are highly structured, meaning the funds must be spent in specific ways, such as hiring staff, marketing, purchasing equipment, or expanding operations. Others come with reporting requirements, where you must submit updates on how you're using the funds.

I remember a large grant I won with a strategic partner. The funding came with strict spending guidelines, and we had to submit quarterly reports detailing exactly where the money went. Every dollar had to be accounted for, from advertising and staff salaries to equipment purchases. We couldn't just spend freely, we had to follow the funder's vision for how the money should be used.

On the other hand, there's something called undesignated funding, and this is the golden ticket of grant funding. These are grants that allow you to allocate the money however you see fit, whether that's paying yourself a salary, hiring staff, or reinvesting in your business. These grants provide the most flexibility because they give you the financial freedom to use the funds in a way that best supports your business or nonprofit.

That being said, there are limits. Grant funding is meant to build, sustain, or expand your business or organization, not fund luxury purchases. You can't take grant money and buy a G-Wagon just because you think it would look good parked in front of your office. Funders want to see responsible financial stewardship, meaning your spending should reflect the mission and goals outlined in your application.

Understanding the different types of grants and their restrictions is crucial to your funding success. In this book, we'll dive deeper into how to find the right grants, how to meet funder expectations, and how to leverage grant funding to build a sustainable business or nonprofit.

WHERE DO GRANTS COME FROM?

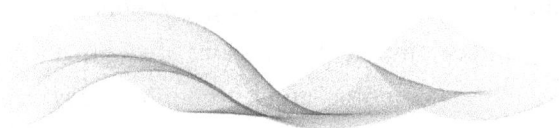

Many people believe that grants only come from the government, but that couldn't be further from the truth. While federal, state, and local governments do offer a wide range of grant opportunities, there are countless other sources of funding available that business owners and nonprofit leaders often overlook.

One of the biggest mistakes I see people make is limiting their search to just one type of grant. The reality is that grants come from multiple sources, and the more you diversify where you look, the greater your chances of securing funding.

When you begin researching grants after reading this book, I encourage you to expand your search beyond government grants and explore opportunities from:

Option 1: State and Local Government Grants – Depending on where you live, your city or state may offer grant programs designed to support small businesses, job creation, economic development, and community-based initiatives. These grants are often less competitive than federal grants, making them an excellent starting point for business owners and nonprofit leaders looking to secure funding.

Option 2: Corporate Grants – Large corporations set aside millions of dollars annually for grant programs designed to support small businesses, nonprofits, and community initiatives. These corporations want to invest in entrepreneurs, women-owned businesses, minority-led ventures, and innovative startups. Some even offer multi-year funding opportunities to help businesses grow over time.

Option 3: Community Grants – Local organizations, economic development programs, and community foundations often provide grants to support small businesses, nonprofits, and community projects. These grants tend to focus on regional impact, making them ideal for local business owners and grassroots initiatives.

Option 4: Private Foundations – Foundations are a major source of grant funding, especially for nonprofits and mission-driven businesses. Many foundations are created by wealthy individuals, families, or companies that want to give back. Some of the most well-known grant funders in this space include the Bill & Melinda Gates Foundation (https://www.gatesfoundation.org), the Ford Foundation (https://www.fordfoundation.org), and the Coca-Cola Foundation (https://www.coca-colacompany.com/social/coca-cola-foundation). However, there are thousands of smaller foundations across the country that offer grants in various industries. In Section 2: Mastering the Grant Application Process, under "Finding Hot Grant Opportunities", I provide detailed information on how to locate these hidden funding sources, research their eligibility criteria, and strategically position yourself to secure funding from them.

Option 5: College and University Grants – Educational institutions frequently offer grants to students, researchers, and business owners who align with their academic or innovation initiatives. Many universities partner with businesses and nonprofit organizations to fund new projects, research, and entrepreneurial ventures.

Option 6: Nonprofit Agencies – Even though nonprofits themselves apply for grants, many also distribute funding to small businesses and entrepreneurs through partnership programs.

Option 7: Small Business Owners & Philanthropists – Believe it or not, many successful entrepreneurs give back to other business owners through grant programs. Some small businesses create their own micro-grants to support startups, women-owned businesses, and underrepresented entrepreneurs. These types of grants may not always be widely advertised, so building relationships and staying connected to your business community can help uncover these hidden opportunities.

TAPPING INTO THESE OPPORTUNITIES

Every one of these entities offers grant funding that you can access, but only if you actively seek out and apply for these opportunities.

I've personally secured funding from nearly all of these sources at some point in my journey. I've won government-funded grants that required detailed proposals and quarterly reporting. I've also been awarded corporate and community grants that had much shorter applications and gave me more flexibility in how I used the funds.

The key is to keep an open mind and diversify where you look for grants. The more you explore, the more opportunities you'll find. And remember, grant funding is not limited to one-time wins. Many organizations offer repeat funding, multi-year grants, and partnerships that can continue supporting your business or nonprofit over time.

As we move through this book, I'll show you exactly how to research, apply for, and secure grants from these different sources so you can build a long-term, sustainable funding strategy.

Grants.gov is Everything

When you visit **www.Grants.gov**, you'll discover one of the most comprehensive platforms for learning about federal grant opportunities. Not only does it list thousands of active grants, but it also offers incredible educational resources, including one of the best Grant Funding Checklists, especially helpful if you're just getting started in the grant funding space.

As you begin your journey of applying for grants, you'll notice that most funders provide a checklist of requirements to help guide you through the application process. In addition, they often follow a structured timeline known as a Grant Cycle.

Here are the key elements of the Grant Cycle:

Element 1: The date they're going to actually have this money available. For example, right now you can find several newspaper articles online that state that Bank of America is putting $3.8 million into women entrepreneurs. You're going to see some sort of announcement in the media.

Element 2: The second thing you're going to see is an open date for grants. That's the date in which you have the opportunity to apply for the grant.

Element 3: The next thing that you're going to see is the close date. That's the date of when the grant application has to be submitted.

Many of you are meeting me for the first time through this book, but I want you to make a commitment to me today. You're going to make a commitment to me today that you're not going to wait until the last minute. Your goal is to get your grant application in early as possible and at least three days before it's due.

I encourage you to submit your grant application early because so many people wait until the very last minute. I've seen folks trying to hit "submit" with just one minute, or even thirty seconds left on the clock. We're not doing that.

We're not putting that kind of stress on ourselves or risking technical issues that could cost us the opportunity. We're committing to excellence and preparation. That means submitting your grant application at least three days in advance to give yourself time, peace of mind, and room for success.

Can I get a commitment from you?

_____Yes _____No

I hope you answered yes.

HOW DO YOU GET GRANT READY?

Before you even think about applying for a grant, you need to take a step back and make sure you are grant ready. Many entrepreneurs and nonprofit leaders dive into the application process without having the foundational elements in place, which often leads to frustration, wasted time, and missed opportunities. Funders are looking to invest in businesses and organizations that have clarity, sustainability, and a strong plan for growth.

I want you to ask yourself this: Is my vision crystal clear?

If someone asked you to explain what your business or nonprofit does, why it exists, and what impact it makes, would you be able to confidently answer? Whether you're seeking funding for a startup, an expansion, a nonprofit project, or even a book, you need to be able to clearly articulate your mission and purpose. Without that clarity, it will be difficult to convince funders why they should invest in you.

GET YOUR BUSINESS PLAN IN ORDER

One of the best ways to solidify your vision is by completing a business plan. This doesn't mean you need a 30-page document with extensive financial projections, even a one-page business plan can provide structure and clarity.

A strong business plan should outline:

- Your mission and vision
- Your target audience and the problem you solve
- Your business or nonprofit goals
- Your revenue model and how you generate income
- Your funding needs and how the grant money will be used

There are countless free one-page business plan templates available online that can help you organize your thoughts and ensure you are presenting your business in a way that funders will take seriously.

KNOW YOUR NUMBERS: BUDGETING FOR GRANT SUCCESS

Your budget is one of the most critical pieces of your grant application. Funders want to see exactly how you plan to use their money. They are not just handing out free cash, they are investing in your business or nonprofit's ability to create impact.

Having a clear and well-organized budget will not only strengthen your application but will also show funders that you understand how to manage money responsibly. If you're unsure how to create a grant budget or need a structured template to guide you, visit https://stan.store/reneebobb-training and download the Grant Funding Budgeting Tool. This tool will help you break down your expenses, categorize your funding needs, and ensure that you are presenting a budget that aligns with the expectations of funders.

When setting up your budget, be specific. Break down exactly where the money will go, whether it's for hiring staff, purchasing equipment, funding a marketing campaign, or launching a new program. The more detailed and transparent you are, the stronger your application will be.

Your budget should also demonstrate financial responsibility. If a funder sees that your numbers are unrealistic or unclear, it raises a red flag.

You need to prove that you can manage the money wisely and that their investment in you will lead to measurable success.

SUSTAINABILITY: WHAT HAPPENS AFTER THE GRANT?

One of the biggest concerns funders have is sustainability. They don't just want to give you money, they want to see that your business or nonprofit will still be standing strong long after the grant funding is spent.

A common question grantors ask is: "How do you make money?" They want to ensure that when the grant period ends, you will still be able to operate, grow, and thrive.

This is why it's essential to have a clear revenue model. Even if you're launching a nonprofit, you need to show that you have diverse income streams, whether through donations, fundraising, partnerships, or earned revenue. If you are a for-profit business, you need to clearly outline your sales strategy and how you plan to scale.

Grant funders are not in the business of saving struggling companies. They are looking to support strong businesses and organizations that have the potential to grow and make an impact. If you can prove that you have a solid plan to generate revenue, sustain your operations, and make their investment worthwhile, your chances of winning funding increase significantly.

THE KEY TO GRANT READINESS

Getting grant ready is about more than just filling out an application. It's about having a clear vision, a solid plan, a well-structured budget, and a sustainable business model.

If you lay the groundwork now, when the right grant opportunity comes along, you'll be fully prepared to submit a winning application. In Section 2: Mastering the Grant Application Process, I will guide you through finding the best grant opportunities, positioning yourself for success, and crafting compelling applications that stand out.

Grant funding isn't just about luck, it's about preparation. When you're grant ready, you don't just chase opportunities, you create them.

CHAPTER 2

MASTERING THE GRANT APPLICATION PROCESS

BUILDING YOUR
PROFESSIONAL TEAM

Securing grant funding isn't just about finding the right opportunities and writing strong applications, it's about having the right team in place to support you throughout the process. The journey to winning grants isn't meant to be walked alone. Successful grant seekers build a professional team of experts, mentors, and strategic partners who help them navigate the complexities of grant funding, ensuring that their applications are strong, their finances are in order, and their projects are well-executed.

When thinking about your dream team, one of the most valuable assets you can have is a strategic nonprofit partner. If you are a business owner, partnering with a nonprofit organization that aligns with your mission can open doors to additional grant funding. Many funders prefer to award grants to businesses that collaborate with nonprofits because it shows a commitment to community impact.

One of my most successful funding strategies has been partnering with nonprofit agencies that offer similar services to mine. Instead of competing for the same pool of funding, I collaborate with them. I help them achieve their mission, and in return, we apply for grants together, increasing our chances of winning.

When I first started seeking business support, I turned to government-funded resources that are designed to help entrepreneurs win grants and grow their businesses, and the best part? These resources are free.

My first step was the Small Business Administration (www.SBA.gov), where staff members are paid to help entrepreneurs like you. My next stop was SCORE (https://www.score.org), a network of business mentors and experts who provide free guidance to business owners. Then, I connected with my local Americas Small Business Development Center (SBDC) https://americassbdc.org/ where specialists are available to help entrepreneurs with marketing plans, business planning, and funding strategies. Every state has an SBDC office, so I encourage you to find the one nearest you.

STRATEGIC PARTNERSHIPS CAN BE A GAME CHANGER

One of the grants I was applying for had a requirement: the applicant must have a PhD. Now, let me tell you, I do not have a PhD. In fact, I barely got my bachelor's degree (but that's a story for another time). Instead of disqualifying myself, I reached out to PhDs in my network who specialized in the area the grant was focused on. I wrote them into the grant proposal as project partners, and when we won the grant, they handled their area of expertise while I managed mine.

This is the power of strategic partnerships. Instead of seeing obstacles, find ways to leverage your network and collaborate with people who meet the grant requirements.

WHY YOU NEED AN ATTORNEY ON YOUR TEAM

Another critical member of your grant funding team should be an attorney. Many grants come with detailed contracts, compliance requirements, and legal terms that you must fully understand before accepting funding.

Every time I win a grant, I have my attorney review the agreement, especially if there is language I don't understand. Some grants may have hidden clauses or obligations that could cause problems down the line if you don't carefully review them.

Remember, you never want to be in a position where you have to return grant money because you didn't meet the requirements. Having a legal expert ensures that you fully understand your obligations and can confidently accept the funding without unexpected risks.

LEVERAGING EXISTING NETWORKS TO MEET GRANT REQUIREMENTS

One of my favorite examples of strategic networking came when AARP (https://www.aarp.org/) launched a grant for programs designed to help individuals aged 50 and older start their own businesses. Recognizing the potential impact of this opportunity, I partnered with a nonprofit organization that applied for the grant, and together, we secured the funding.

What made this grant unique was that AARP had already developed comprehensive training materials, eliminating the need for me to create content from scratch. My primary role was to outline how I would effectively reach the target audience. Instead of spending valuable time and resources trying to build an audience from the ground up, I took a different approach, I leveraged existing networks that were already engaged with the 50-and-older community.

I connected with church ministries that had programs specifically designed for older adults, ensuring that I could tap into a community that was already invested in entrepreneurship and personal development. I also partnered with a well-established nonprofit organization that serves individuals aged 55 and older, offering resources, programs, and support tailored to their needs. Additionally, I reached out to various community organizations that were already working closely with this demographic, making it easy to integrate the AARP program into their existing outreach efforts.

By demonstrating that we had access to a built-in audience, our application stood out. AARP saw that we had a well-thought-out plan, credible partnerships, and a direct pipeline to the people they wanted to reach. This made them confident that we could successfully deliver the program and maximize the impact of their funding.

The lesson here? You don't always have to create something new to secure grant funding. Sometimes, the smartest strategy is tapping into networks that already exist. By aligning with organizations that have established credibility and a built-in audience, you strengthen your grant application and increase your chances of success.

FINANCIAL EXPERTS TO KEEP YOU COMPLIANT

Many grants require recipients to report back on how they spent the money, which is why having a bookkeeper, accountant, or tax professional as part of your team is essential. Proper financial management ensures that you remain compliant with the funder's requirements and avoid any issues that could jeopardize future funding opportunities.

A good accountant or bookkeeper will establish a clear financial tracking system that categorizes your grant expenses, making it easy to monitor where every dollar is allocated. When it's time to submit reports, instead of scrambling to gather receipts and justify expenditures, you simply generate a detailed report at the push of a button. This level of organization not only saves time but also strengthens your credibility with funders, showing them that you are a responsible steward of their investment.

If you're managing your finances yourself, using QuickBooks (https:// quickbooks.intuit.com/) or a similar accounting tool can help you stay organized. However, if numbers aren't your strength, hiring a professional is a smart investment. Having an expert on your team ensures that your financial records are accurate, your reporting is seamless, and you're always prepared for any funding opportunities that require strong financial documentation.

If you're seeking alternatives to QuickBooks, several accounting software options are available that cater to diverse business needs and budgets.

HoneyBook
https://www.honeybook.com

Ideal for small businesses and entrepreneurs. HoneyBook streamlines invoicing, payment processing, and financial tracking with an intuitive interface. It's particularly useful for service-based businesses.

FreshBooks
https://www.freshbooks.com

A great choice for freelancers and small business owners, FreshBooks offers easy-to-use accounting tools, automated invoicing, expense tracking, and financial reporting.

Wave
https://www.waveapps.com

A free accounting software solution that provides bookkeeping, invoicing, and expense tracking. It's an excellent option for startups and small businesses looking for a budget-friendly alternative.

Xero
https://www.xero.com

A powerful cloud-based accounting tool with robust financial tracking, automated bank reconciliations, and integration with various business apps. Xero is great for businesses that need scalable financial management.

Zoho Books
https://www.zoho.com/books

Zoho suite is an accounting software is designed for small businesses and provides financial reporting, tax compliance, and expense tracking, making it a great all-in-one solution.

Each of these platforms offers unique features, so the best choice depends on your business needs, budget, and level of accounting expertise.

THE ROLE OF SOCIAL MEDIA IN GRANT FUNDING

You may not realize it, but social media can play a huge role in whether or not you win certain grants. Some grants, like the FedEx Small Business Grant, are based on public voting. The more votes you receive, the higher your chances of winning.

Having a strong social media presence can give you a competitive edge. If you have a dedicated social media strategist on your team, they can help you promote your grant applications, generate engagement, and drive votes, which could be the difference between winning and losing.

Additionally, many grant funders review your social media pages before awarding funding. They want to verify that your business is active, aligned with your mission, and engaging with your audience. They'll also visit your website to see if your branding and messaging reflect what you wrote in your application.

Make sure your social media pages and website are not only professional and polished but also reflect the story you're telling in your grant proposals. Funders want to see that your digital presence is consistent with your mission, values, and the impact you've outlined in your application. A strong and authentic online presence can reinforce your credibility and in some cases, tip the scales in your favor.

THE IMPORTANCE OF BUILDING A RELATIONSHIP WITH YOUR BANKER

One often-overlooked member of your professional team is your banker. Your bank isn't just a place to deposit money, it's a resource for financial advice, funding opportunities, and networking connections.

Bankers are often aware of grant programs, sponsorships, and other funding resources that may not be widely advertised. They can also help you build and strengthen your business credit, which can unlock even more financial opportunities down the line.

If you haven't already established a relationship with your banker, now is the perfect time to start. A trusted banking partner can become a valuable ally in your funding journey.

THE ROLE OF A PROFESSIONAL EDITOR IN YOUR GRANT APPLICATIONS

Before you even think about hiring a grant writer, there's one essential role you don't want to overlook, a professional editor. While grant writers help you craft your message, editors ensure that message is clean, powerful, and professionally presented. This step is often skipped, but it can be the difference between a winning application and one that gets passed over.

When you're passionate about your business or nonprofit, it's easy to overlook small errors. I can't tell you how many times I've typed "there" when I really meant "their." These little mistakes might seem minor, but to a funder, they can reflect a lack of attention to detail. That's why I always have a professional editor review my grant applications before I hit submit.

Your grant proposal needs to be polished, professional, and error-free. A good editor ensures your writing is clear, persuasive, and grammatically correct. They help refine your message without changing your voice, making sure you're communicating with clarity and confidence. In a competitive grant pool, those small refinements can significantly impact how funders perceive your application, and ultimately, whether you get funded.

While hiring a grant writer can be helpful, I encourage you to learn the basics of grant writing yourself. Even if you eventually outsource the process, having a strong understanding of what funders are looking for will make you a better applicant.

YOUR DREAM TEAM IS YOUR KEY TO GRANT SUCCESS

Winning grant funding is a team effort. Surrounding yourself with the right experts, partners, and advisors will make your funding journey smoother, more efficient, and more successful. By building a strategic, well-rounded team, you're not just increasing your chances of securing funding, you're setting yourself up for long-term business success.

HOW TO FIND A PROFESSIONAL GRANT WRITER?

Finding the right grant writer can be one of the best investments you make for your business or nonprofit. A skilled professional can help you craft compelling proposals, stay compliant with funder requirements, and increase your chances of securing grant funding. Below are current and effective strategies to help you locate an experienced and trustworthy grant writer.

OPTION 1: CHECK WITH LOCAL COLLEGES AND UNIVERSITIES

Reach out to your local college or university, particularly the English, Journalism, Public Administration, or Nonprofit Management departments. Many schools have faculty or advanced students with grant writing experience, and some even offer grant writing as part of their curriculum or professional development programs.

OPTION 2: CONNECT WITH NONPROFIT RESOURCE CENTERS

Many cities have nonprofit resource centers or community foundations that provide referrals to grant writers or offer grant writing workshops. One

example is the **Center for Nonprofit Management** (Nashville-based). Check to see if a similar organization operates in your region.
https://www.cnm.org

OPTION 3: USE THE GRANT PROFESSIONALS ASSOCIATION DIRECTORY

The **Grant Professionals Association (GPA)** is a national organization of credentialed grant writers. Their searchable member directory allows you to find certified grant writers by state or area of expertise.
https://grantprofessionals.org

OPTION 4: RESEARCH THE AMERICAN GRANT WRITERS' ASSOCIATION (AGWA)

AGWA offers training, certification, and a referral directory for professional grant writers. This is a great place to find writers with experience in federal, state, and private grant proposals.
http://www.agwa.us/

OPTION 5: USE FREELANCE PLATFORMS FOR GRANT WRITERS

Professional freelancers often offer grant writing services on trusted freelance platforms. Make sure to check reviews, ratings, and examples of previous work:

- **Upwork**: https://www.upwork.com
- **Fiverr**: https://www.fiverr.com
- **PeoplePerHour**: https://www.peopleperhour.com

These platforms allow you to compare pricing, read reviews, and select professionals who match your budget and needs.

OPTION 6: CONTACT YOUR LOCAL CHAMBER OF COMMERCE

Your local Chamber may have a directory of small businesses and service providers, including grant writers or consultants. Chambers are great for making local business-to-business connections and finding trusted service providers.

OPTION 7: REACH OUT TO CHURCHES AND COMMUNITY DEVELOPMENT CORPORATIONS (CDCS)

Many churches, particularly larger ones, operate CDCs that are involved in grant-funded community initiatives. Someone on staff may either offer grant writing services or be able to refer you to a trusted contact.

OPTION 8: ATTEND NETWORKING EVENTS OR JOIN BUSINESS GROUPS

Whether virtual or in-person, business expos, entrepreneur meetups, non-profit summits, and small business roundtables are great places to meet grant professionals. Let people know you're actively looking, and ask for referrals, you'll often find hidden gems through word of mouth.

OPTION 9: SEARCH ONLINE FOR "AWARD-WINNING GRANT WRITERS NEAR ME"

Sometimes, a simple Google search can surface experienced professionals in your area who have been recognized for their success with large foundations or government grants. Look for those with client testimonials, successful case studies, or media coverage.

BONUS TIP:

If you're unsure where to start, try searching LinkedIn using keywords like *"Certified Grant Writer," "Federal Grant Consultant,"* or *"Nonprofit Funding Strategist"*. LinkedIn makes it easy to see mutual connections, endorsements, and client recommendations.

FINDING HOT GRANT OPPORTUNITIES

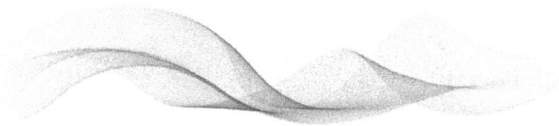

One of the most important keys to securing consistent grant funding is knowing where to look. Gone are the days of just relying on Google searches or outdated grant directories. In today's digital world, you need to tap into live databases, niche platforms, and trusted networks that consistently deliver results. If you're serious about finding grant opportunities that match your mission and vision, it's time to level up your strategy.

Here's the process I now teach inside my training and programs, and it's one that has helped thousands of my clients successfully secure grants and business capital:

Nonprofit and Corporate Grant Directory
https://corporategrantsguide.com/business-directory/wpbdp_category/charitable-giving/?wpbdp_sort=field-11

Start with the Nonprofit and Corporate Grant Directory hosted by Corporate Grants Guide. This powerful resource offers a searchable business directory featuring hundreds of charitable giving programs. It's updated regularly and is a goldmine for nonprofit agencies and businesses that align with corporate social impact initiatives.

F6S

https://www.f6s.com/programs

Next, head over to F6S, which houses one of the most comprehensive and active lists of accelerators, pitch competitions, and business development programs across the globe. These opportunities often come with funding, resources, and investor access, which is perfect for scaling your business or launching a new product.

Novae Grants Portal

https://grants.Novaegrants.com/

For a centralized grant database tailored for small businesses, nonprofits, and creatives, use the Novae Grants Portal. This system gives you access to real-time funding opportunities and is updated weekly.

In addition to those top three tools, here are a few other high-performing platforms that consistently produce funding wins for my clients:

Grantwatch.com – A long-time trusted platform for both business and nonprofit grant seekers.
https://www.grantwatch.com/

Candid's Foundation Directory – Great for locating foundation-based funding and private family foundation grants.
https://candid.org/find-nonprofit-funding

Community Foundations – Every state has several, and they fund hyper-local businesses and programs.

Economic Development Organizations – Your city or region may offer grants and incentives you haven't tapped into yet.

For niche grants and creative funding:

- **Grantsforwomen.org** – A curated list of opportunities for women entrepreneurs.
  https://www.grantsforwomen.org/p/opportunities-grants-for-women-ab.Html

- **Hello Alice** – One of the most popular platforms offering ongoing small business grant rounds.
  https://auth.helloalice.com/

- **Hello Skip** – Offers funding updates, alerts, and personal assistance for grants, credit, and business growth.
  https://helloskip.com/sign-in?ref=RENEE145

- **U.S. Chamber of Commerce** – Maintains a live guide of federal, state, and private business grant programs.
  https://www.uschamber.com/co/run/business-financing/government-small-business-grant-programs

BONUS STRATEGY: SOCIAL LISTENING & NETWORKING STILL WINS

While databases and platforms are essential, never underestimate the power of social media and relationship-building. Follow banks, celebrities, local businesses, and major brands on platforms like Instagram, LinkedIn, and Facebook, these are often the first places they post when a new grant opens.

If you see another entrepreneur or nonprofit post about winning a grant, don't scroll past it. Go to the source. Research the program, follow the funder, and see if the opportunity is recurring. Winning often comes down to being in the right place at the right time, and staying connected makes sure you are.

Also, always reverse-engineer where the money flows. Shop at Kroger? Go to Kroger's social impact or foundation page. Use Verizon? Look at their grant initiatives. Drive a Toyota? Toyota funds local and national community projects. If you're spending money with a brand, there's a good chance they're giving some of it back to the community, and possibly to you.

The landscape of funding has evolved, and now you have access to smarter tools and targeted strategies. Combine these resources with your passion and purpose, and you'll build your own custom grant funding list that delivers real results all year long.

THE PSYCHOLOGY OF FUNDERS: UNDERSTANDING WHAT GRANTORS WANT

Securing grant funding goes far beyond writing a strong proposal, it requires a deep understanding of the people behind the dollars. Funders are not just institutions or faceless organizations; they are mission-driven individuals and committees who are passionate about specific causes and outcomes. To win grants consistently, you must align your vision with theirs and present your project in a way that speaks directly to their motivations.

FUNDERS ARE LOOKING FOR IMPACT

At the core, funders want to know: What problem are you solving, and how effectively will you solve it? They invest in transformation. Whether you're helping women start businesses, educating youth, or expanding access to healthcare, funders want to see tangible, measurable change. They want stories. They want data. They want both the *heart* and the *proof* that your work matters.

FUNDERS VALUE ALIGNMENT WITH THEIR MISSION

Every grantor has a unique mission and set of values. Some focus on economic empowerment, others on racial equity, youth development, or innovation in technology. A funder's mission is their "why." When you apply for a grant, your first job is to *study the funder* and make sure your application aligns with their purpose. When a funder reads your proposal and sees their mission reflected back to them, that's when the magic happens.

FUNDERS WANT TO FEEL CONFIDENT IN YOU

Confidence builds trust, and funders want to trust that you'll follow through. This is where your preparation, professionalism, and track record matter. Even if you're a startup, demonstrating a solid plan, strong leadership, clear financials, and community support gives funders the reassurance they need to say "yes." Ask yourself: *If I were investing $25,000 in someone's dream, what would I want to see?* That's the mindset shift.

FUNDERS ARE STRATEGIC PARTNERS

Today's funders want more than transactional relationships, they seek transformation and partnership. They want to fund entrepreneurs and nonprofits that reflect their commitment to systemic change. When you position yourself as a partner, not just an applicant, you create an opportunity for long-term support, mentorship, and collaboration.

Be transparent. Be authentic. Be open to feedback. Funders remember organizations that communicate well, follow up, and show gratitude.

Understanding the psychology of funders helps you write stronger applications, build better relationships, and increase your chances of funding success. Funders want to fund YOU, your vision, your mission, your impact. The more you learn to speak their language, the more doors you will open.

HOW TO PITCH YOUR BUSINESS OR NONPROFIT FOR GRANT FUNDING

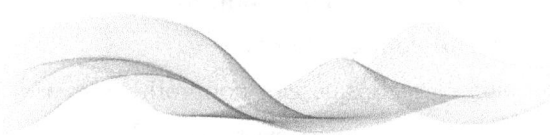

Great example: Tanya Walker stood nervously in front of the funders, her palms slightly damp, heart racing. She was at a grant pitch competition in Atlanta, and she had exactly three minutes to share her story, her impact, and her vision. Her nonprofit, *Moms Who Code*, had already helped dozens of single mothers learn software development and land high-paying remote jobs, but today was about more than numbers. Today was about connection. As the clock started ticking, Tanya took a deep breath and spoke the words that changed everything.

"Three years ago, I was working two jobs, raising two kids, and one step away from eviction. Everything changed when I learned to code. Now, I'm helping other moms do the same."

In just a few words, she drew the audience in. She made them feel her journey. She painted a clear picture of the problem; single mothers trapped in low-wage jobs with no clear pathway out, and offered a powerful solution: tech training and job placement for a vulnerable yet determined population. By the time she finished, she had clearly laid out the scope of her impact, sharing that 83% of her graduates found jobs within six months. She ended her pitch with a confident ask for $25,000 to scale the program to three additional cities. Tanya walked away with more than just funding; she walked away with new partners, media exposure, and the fuel to keep going.

What Tanya did so effectively was speak to both the heart and the mind of the funders. That's the secret of a powerful pitch, it's not just about rattling off facts or explaining your business plan. It's about clearly communicating why your work matters and how the funder's investment will help magnify that impact. Funders want to see that you understand the community you serve, that you've built something meaningful, and that you have a plan to grow. They want to feel your passion, see your preparedness, and trust your execution.

When you pitch your business or nonprofit, start with the mission, what drives you and why your work exists. Then, bring that mission to life through story. Share the real-world transformations your organization or company has helped make possible. Let them hear the voices of the people you've helped. Once you've connected emotionally, follow through with the data; your reach, your results, and your plans. Funders are inspired by purpose, but they're motivated by proof.

And when you make your ask, be specific. Don't assume funders will figure out how much you need or how you'll use it. Be clear, confident, and direct. Show that you've thought it through, and explain exactly how the funds will be spent and how success will be measured. It also helps to remember that pitching isn't just a one-time presentation, it's the beginning of a relationship. Funders remember those who follow up, show appreciation, and continue to share the progress and impact of the work they've supported.

Tanya's story reminds us that pitching is both an art and a strategy. When done right, it can unlock not just funding, but connection, credibility, and opportunity. So, the next time you're in front of a funder, whether in a boardroom, on Zoom, or at a community event, know your story, believe in your vision, and speak with purpose. Because your next three-minute window might just change everything.

CTION STEP: CRAFT YOUR WINNING PITCH

Now it's your turn. Take the time to craft a compelling three-minute pitch for your business or nonprofit. Use the structure below to guide your message. Write it out, rehearse it, and practice delivering it with confidence and passion.

Step 1: Start with your "why." Share a brief personal story or experience that led to the creation of your business or nonprofit. Let your passion shine through.

_____

_____

_____

_____

_____

_____

Step 2: Define the problem. Clearly articulate the issue your business or organization is solving. Help the listener understand why this problem matters.

_____

_____

_____

_____

_____

_____

Step 3: Present your solution. Explain how your product, program, or service addresses the problem in a meaningful and effective way.

_____

_____

_____

_____

_____

_____

_____

Step 4: Show your impact. Use real numbers, testimonials, or outcomes to demonstrate the difference you've made, or the potential impact if you're just getting started.

_____

_____

_____

_____

_____

_____

_____

_____

Step 5: Make the ask. Clearly state how much funding you're seeking, what the funds will be used for, and what results you expect to achieve with the support.

_____

_____

_____

_____

_____

_____

_____

_____

Once you've written your pitch, say it out loud. Record yourself, refine the delivery, and practice until it feels natural. Then, share it with a mentor, friend, or coach for feedback. Remember, your story is powerful and when told with clarity and confidence, it can open doors you never imagined.

THE SECRET TO GRANT WRITING SUCCESS

One of the most powerful secrets to grant writing success today is mastering the art of storytelling, and I'm not just talking about sharing a few facts or accomplishments. I mean telling a story that moves hearts, shifts perspectives, and positions you and your business or nonprofit as the *only* choice for the funding. Whether you're applying for a grant, preparing for a pitch competition, or entering a business plan contest, your story is your currency. It's the key that unlocks opportunities.

So, what are you going to say in that grant application that's going to get the funder's attention? What's going to compel them to believe that your story is worth investing in? That's what you need to uncover and articulate with clarity and conviction.

Let me make it plain: people fund purpose. Your purpose must be felt, understood, and backed by a plan of action. Funders aren't just reviewing your budgets, they're reviewing your belief system, your commitment to impact, and your ability to deliver real results.

Your story needs to show the problem you're solving and the transformation that will happen when you're funded. What will you do with the money? How will lives be changed? Communities impacted? Systems improved? That's what grantors are looking for.

Let's pause here and dig into your unique story. Use the space below to reflect and write:

1. What are you going to say in your grant application that clearly communicates your story and sells funders on your vision?

_____

_____

_____

_____

_____

_____

2. What will make your story so powerful, so undeniable, that funders know you are the perfect fit for the grant?

_____

_____

_____

_____

_____

_____

When I review successful grant proposals, I look deeper than just their structure or formatting, I analyze the emotional undertone, the clarity of their mission, and how they communicate impact. I always ask myself: *What is it about their story that made someone want to write a check?* That level of insight can only come from studying winners and identifying the thread that ties them all together, a compelling story rooted in purpose and potential.

Now, I'm not saying to copy someone else's story. But you can absolutely study what works and ask yourself how to incorporate that level of excellence into your own grant writing process. Learn from those who are winning and elevate your approach.

This is why I often recommend working with a great content writer or grant strategist. Yes, you can write your story on your own, but sometimes you need someone who knows how to bring out the *essence* of your mission. A skilled writer will help you identify the golden pieces of your journey that funders need to see and feel. Your story is already powerful you just need to frame it right.

Another powerful secret? Study winning grant proposals. Make that part of your research strategy. You can find samples online, request examples from local nonprofits or entrepreneurs, or ask foundations if they're willing to share successful applications. The structure, tone, and language they use can give your insight into how to make your proposals stand out.

And if you apply for a grant and don't win, follow up! Most people don't, and that's a missed opportunity. Contact the funder. Ask for feedback. Understand what you could improve. That kind of feedback is gold. It sharpens your next application and shows funders that you're committed to growth.

Also, don't underestimate the right resources in your community. Your local library, economic development office, and community foundations often have directories, guides, and even grant workshops available. They may even have grant writing books broken down by state or industry. All of that is valuable when building your strategy.

And here's the truth: if you don't have the time or bandwidth to do this work, you need to build a team or delegate the task. Whether it's hiring a researcher, bringing in a VA, or finding someone to help manage your deadlines, you don't have to do it all alone. But it *must* get done because the funding is out there, and the resources are waiting for you.

So, it's time. No more waiting. No more wondering. It's time to apply. Use the Grant Funding Resource Directory at the back of this book to get started. Choose three grants to apply for this month and start telling your story like your funding depends on it and because and it does.

Let's go get this money.
You've got everything you need.

CHAPTER 3

AI & TECHNOLOGY IN GRANT FUNDING

AI TOOLS FOR FINDING AND WRITING GRANTS

Welcome to the future of funding. Artificial Intelligence (AI) is no longer just a high-tech buzzword, it's a strategic advantage for small business owners and nonprofit leaders. Today, AI tools are revolutionizing the way we search for grants, write proposals, track deadlines, and ensure compliance. If you've ever felt overwhelmed by the grant process, AI can help you save time, reduce stress, and increase your success rate.

This section of the guide will help you unlock the power of AI in your grant funding journey, whether you're just getting started or looking to scale.

HOW AI IS CHANGING THE GRANT FUNDING LANDSCAPE

AI is transforming every step of the grant process. From automating repetitive tasks to generating full-length draft proposals, AI is making it easier to stay organized, access relevant funding opportunities, and tailor your applications to funder priorities.

Instead of spending 10 hours researching grants, you can now have AI scan databases and provide a list of the most relevant opportunities in minutes. AI can summarize guidelines, highlight key requirements, and even help you avoid costly mistakes in your application. It's like having a full-time research assistant, proposal writer, and grant strategist rolled into one.

LEVERAGING DATA & AUTOMATION FOR SMARTER GRANT APPLICATIONS

Smart grant seekers don't just guess, they use data. AI tools allow you to analyze what types of projects are getting funded, what language resonates with funders, and which funders align best with your mission.

Automation also ensures that you never miss a deadline or skip an important document. With the right tools, you can build out systems that send reminders, autofill repetitive information, and store your grant history, so you're always one step ahead.

USING AI FOR GRANT RESEARCH, PROPOSAL WRITING & COMPLIANCE

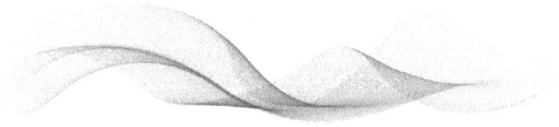

The biggest value of AI? Efficiency and precision. You can now use tools like ChatGPT, Claude, and Gemini to generate proposal drafts, check your writing for tone and clarity, summarize funder priorities, and even ensure you're meeting compliance standards.

Need to find a grant focused on STEM education for women in rural communities? AI can help you locate it in seconds. Not sure how to structure your budget narrative? Ask the AI. Wondering if your proposal aligns with a funder's mission? Use AI to analyze the language on their website and match it to your proposal.

INTRODUCTION TO CHATGPT

One of the most powerful AI tools available today is **ChatGPT**, (https:// chat.openai.com) developed by OpenAI. ChatGPT is an advanced language model designed to simulate real conversations and provide information, draft content, solve problems, and help you think creatively. In short, it's like having a grant coach, strategist, and assistant right at your fingertips—24/7.

SHOULD I USE AI?

If you want to save time, enhance your writing, find more grant opportunities, and stay organized, then yes. Using AI doesn't mean replacing your judgment; it means strengthening your grant strategy. The most successful organizations are already leveraging AI to increase capacity and results. If you want to stay competitive, now is the time to adopt these tools.

WHAT IS CHATGPT?

ChatGPT is a conversational AI tool that allows you to type questions and receive human-like responses in real-time. You can ask it to help you write a grant proposal, review your eligibility, summarize funding guidelines, or even role-play as a funder reviewing your application.

WHAT IS PROMPT ENGINEERING?

Prompt Engineering is the art and strategy of asking the right questions in the right way to get powerful, helpful, and specific responses from AI tools. The better your prompt, the better the result. Think of it as giving clear instructions to your digital assistant.

SECRET: CHATGPT IS DESIGNED TO HAVE A CONVERSATION

Here's the secret: ChatGPT works best when you treat it like a conversation partner. Ask follow-up questions. Clarify your intent. Build on each answer. The more you engage, the more helpful and customized the responses become.

AI TOOLS TO FIND OPPORTUNITIES

Here are some top AI tools you can use to find and apply for grant funding:

1. DeepSeek – https://www.deepseek.com
An advanced AI search engine that helps you find funding opportunities, research partners, and data sources across a wide variety of industries and sectors. Great for deep-dive grant discovery.

2. ChatGPT – https://chatgpt.com
Perfect for grant writing, idea generation, research summaries, proposal editing, and follow-up communication templates. You can even role-play a grant reviewer to improve your proposals.

3. Claude – https://claude.ai
Created by Anthropic, Claude is an AI assistant known for its ethical training and natural conversational tone. It's great for writing in a warm, human voice, perfect for storytelling in your proposals.

4. Gemini (by Google) – https://gemini.google.com
Formerly Bard, Gemini is a robust AI system with deep integration into Google tools. Excellent for collaboration, document editing, and real-time research support inside Google Docs or Gmail.

HOW TO USE PROMPT
ENGINEERING EFFECTIVELY

Here are ten simple strategies to help you master prompt engineering:

1. **Be Clear and Specific with Your Questions.** Instead of asking "Help me write a grant," ask, "Can you write a 500-word grant proposal for a nonprofit that supports youth entrepreneurship in Chicago?"

2. **Break Down Complex Requests.** Instead of overwhelming prompts, ask step-by-step. Start with: "Help me write the needs statement," then move to "Now write the program description."

3. **Use Follow-Up Questions.** After receiving a draft, say: "Can you rewrite this section to sound more compelling?" or "Make this paragraph more data-driven."

4. **Leverage My Expertise Across Topics.** Ask ChatGPT to compare funding opportunities, summarize federal vs. state grants, or generate marketing content to promote your funded program.

5. **Ask for Templates, Scripts, or Examples.** Need a capability statement? Email to a funder? AI can draft them all.

6. **Use Me for Brainstorming.** Stuck on an idea? Ask ChatGPT to brainstorm names for your program, funding angles, or impact strategies.

7. **Request Summaries or Action Plans.** Don't get overwhelmed. Ask: "Summarize this 10-page grant guide into key steps," or "Give me a 5-day plan to complete this grant."

8. **Take Notes and Save Responses.** Use ChatGPT to keep track of deadlines, ideas, or funder notes. Copy and save conversations for future grants.

9. **Experiment and Try Different Requests.** Don't be afraid to tweak your approach. Sometimes a simple rephrase gives you a stronger result.

10. **Have Fun and Explore.** AI isn't just business, it's creative too! Use it to visualize your project's future, imagine your pitch, or write an award acceptance speech (claim it early!).

The P.R.I.D.E. System for Prompting ChatGPT

To help you get the most out of ChatGPT and other AI tools, use the **P.R.I.D.E. System**:

P – Parameters: Set boundaries like word count, tone, or emotion. Example: "Keep the response under 300 words. Use persuasive, confident language."

R – Role: Assign the AI a role. Example: "Act like a seasoned Grant Writer with over 10 years of experience." This helps the AI understand the perspective and tone it should use.

I – Instructions: Be clear about what you want it to do. Example: "Review this grant proposal and suggest edits for clarity and impact."

D – Desired Outcome: Define what success looks like or what you want to walk away with.
Example: "I want a compelling pitch paragraph I can use for my grant application." This helps ChatGPT focus on delivering exactly what you need, whether it's a polished document, a list of resources, or a clear step-by-step action plan.

E – Example: Provide context or reference materials. Example: "Here is my website and capability statement. Use this info in the grant narrative."

Note: Each conversation/chat is saved. You can refer back to it later as you continue applying for grants.

SAMPLE PROMPT
YOU CAN TRY

"Act like a seasoned Grant Writer with over 10 years of experience. I run a nonprofit that provides after-school STEM programs to underserved youth in Baltimore. Write a compelling 300-word grant narrative that includes our mission, the problem we solve, our solution, and the impact we've made. Keep the tone confident, passionate, and professional."

This is how you start crafting powerful content with the help of AI tools.

Remember: The future of funding belongs to those who adapt, innovate, and take bold steps. AI is not replacing your brilliance, it's here to amplify it. Learn the tools, use the system, and start winning with confidence.

Are you ready to level up?

Here are a few optimized AI prompts, each crafted to generate strong, detailed, and emotionally engaging responses when used with tools like ChatGPT or Claude. These prompts follow the P.R.I.D.E. method and are designed to help your clients, students, or readers produce powerful content for grant applications, pitch competitions, or business storytelling.

Question 1: How would you describe your business? What are the products and/or services you offer? (Max 300 words)

Prompt to Use:

Act like a seasoned grant writer and brand strategist. I need a 300-word business description that clearly explains what my business does, who it serves, and the products or services we offer. The tone should be professional, confident, and clear. Please structure the response to include: (1) the name and mission of the business, (2) the target audience or customer base, (3) a breakdown of the main products/services, and (4) a sentence or two about how we stand out in the marketplace. Here's my business info: [Insert brief details about your business].

Question 2: What is the biggest obstacle or challenge that your business will face this year?

Prompt to Use:

Act like a small business consultant and grant application expert. I need help writing a 200-word explanation of the biggest obstacle my business is facing this year. The tone should be honest yet hopeful. Please explain the challenge, how it affects our operations, and what we're doing (or planning) to overcome it. Here's what we're currently struggling with: [Insert brief description of the obstacle].

Question 3: Why did you become a small business owner? What is the origin story of your business? Please be as specific as possible.

Prompt to Use:

Act like a storytelling coach and professional content writer. Help me write the origin story of my business in 300 words or less. I want to explain why I became a business owner, what personal or professional experiences led me to start the business, and how that journey connects to the mission we serve today. The tone should be inspiring, heartfelt, and specific. Here's a brief outline of my story: [Insert a few sentences about your background and motivation].

Question 4: What Will You Use This Grant For?

Prompt to Use:

Act like a grant writer with experience winning funding for small businesses. Help me write a clear, detailed response explaining how I will use a grant (up to $10,000) to grow or sustain my business. Please include specific expenses (e.g., equipment, marketing, staffing, training, product development), the impact of the grant on our growth or community, and how we'll measure success. Here's a breakdown of what I'd like to use the grant for: [Insert your budget or priority needs].

CHAPTER 4

DIVERSE FUNDING STRATEGIES FOR BUSINESS OWNERS & NONPROFITS

DIVERSE FUNDING STRATEGIES FOR BUSINESS OWNERS & NONPROFITS

Securing funding is about more than just applying for grants, it's about understanding the full spectrum of financial resources available to help your business or nonprofit grow, thrive, and create lasting impact. In this chapter, we're diving into diverse funding strategies beyond traditional grants, including crowdfunding, corporate sponsorships, business plan competitions, pitch opportunities, and how to find Requests for Proposals (RFPs). These are all powerful options that can open new doors for funding, visibility, and partnership.

As you explore the resources and links provided throughout this chapter, please note that websites and URLs are constantly being updated or changed. If you click on a link and it doesn't work, don't get discouraged. Simply copy and paste the name of the grant, program, or resource into your Google search bar or ChatGPT, and you should be able to locate the most current and updated link.

We have done our absolute best to verify each link and ensure it's accurate and working at the time of publication. Your success matters to us, and we want to make sure you have the tools and knowledge to find and secure every funding opportunity available to you.

Let's explore these powerful strategies together, and discover the many ways you can fund your vision.

Instructions on how to use this Grant list:

Step 1: Review the List

- Carefully read through the descriptions provided for each grant.
- Click on the "Apply Here" link next to each grant to visit the respective application page.
- Verify your eligibility by reviewing the grant requirements listed on the application page.

Step 2: Research Additional Opportunities

- Take your time to thoroughly explore sites like Grants.gov and other similar platforms.
- These websites have extensive databases of grants that you may qualify for, but it requires patience and diligence to identify suitable opportunities.

Step 3: Prioritize Grants by Deadline

- Once you have a clear understanding of the grants you qualify for, organize them based on their application deadlines.
- Create a timeline or calendar to manage and track your application process effectively. Be sure to use the Grant Funding Tracking Form located in the resource section of this book.

Step 4: Apply Consistently

- Set a goal to apply for at least three grants each week.
- Ensure that you tailor each application to meet the specific requirements of the grant and provide all necessary documentation.

Step 5: Seek Assistance if Needed

- If you encounter any difficulties or have questions about the application process, do not hesitate to reach out for help.
- You can contact me directly at www.ReneeBobbTraining.com for support and guidance.

Important Disclaimer:

- Be aware that legitimate grant applications will never ask for your social security number, money, a copy of your driver's license, or banking information during the application process.
- When you are awarded a grant, the funding will typically be provided through a secure portal, direct deposit the funds or mailed as a check.

General Disclaimer:

- The information provided in this Grant Funding List is intended for general informational purposes only.
- Neither Renee Bobb nor Renee Bobb Training LLC makes any representations or warranties, express or implied, regarding the accuracy, completeness, or reliability of the information.
- Your use of the grant information and any linked third-party content is solely at your own risk.
- We do not endorse or assume any liability for third-party content. It is essential to conduct your own due diligence and research before applying for any grant.

Additional Tips:

- Keep a record of all the grants you apply for, including submission dates and any follow-up actions required.
- Review and update your grant application materials regularly to ensure they reflect your most recent achievements and organizational needs.
- Consider seeking feedback on your applications from peers or mentors to improve your chances of success.

By following these steps and tips, you can effectively navigate the grant application process and increase your chances of securing funding for your projects and initiatives.

TOP 12 OPTIONS TO
FINANCE YOUR DREAM

When it comes to funding your business or nonprofit, you must adopt a new mindset: stop relying solely on your own money. Starting today, make a commitment to explore and pursue external funding sources. Why? Because the money is out there, millions of dollars in grant funding, pitch competitions, business credit, and sponsorships are available to those who know how to find and leverage them.

I say this all the time, you don't have to fund your vision alone. Whether you're just starting or looking to scale, there are smarter, more strategic ways to get the capital you need. One pitch competition or grant can completely transform your business. I've seen it happen time and time again.

Take pitch competitions, for example. One of my favorite ways to secure funding quickly is by entering well-aligned pitch contests. These aren't just for tech startups, businesses in every industry are winning thousands of dollars to grow and scale. Platforms like F6S offer an up-to-date list of pitch competitions and accelerators around the world. I recommend visiting https://www.f6s.com/programs and keeping your eye on upcoming contests.

And when you pitch, clarity is key. Judges may not know your industry, so your message needs to be clear, concise, and impactful, at a 7th-grade level. If they don't understand what you do or how the money will be used, they won't fund you. I encourage you to watch successful pitch competitions on YouTube. Study the delivery, storytelling, and confidence of past winners, then practice and refine your own pitch strategy until it resonates with clarity and conviction.

In addition to grants and pitch contests, here are several viable funding options to consider as you build and expand your business:

1. **Business Credit & Lines of Credit** – Establishing strong business credit can help you access funding without personal guarantees.

2. **Crowdfunding Platforms** – Sites like IFundWomen and Kickstarter allow you to raise capital from your community and beyond.

3. **Corporate Sponsorships** – Partner with brands that align with your mission; many offer sponsorship dollars to support minority, veteran, or women-owned businesses.

4. **Venture Capital & Angel Investors** – Especially for scalable, high-impact businesses, equity investors can be a strategic funding source.

5. **Community and Faith-Based Groups** – Local organizations, churches, and community development funds often support entrepreneurs creating change.

6. **Business Plan & Pitch Competitions** – Whether virtual or in-person, these competitions offer cash prizes and exposure.

7. **Government & Private Grants** – As covered throughout this book, grants are one of the most powerful ways to access non-repayable funding.

8. **Strategic Partnerships** – Collaborate with nonprofits, agencies, or businesses on joint ventures that receive funding together.

9. **Family and Friends** – If they believe in your vision, they may be willing to support your launch or growth. Just make sure the terms are clear.

10. **Digital Product Sales** – Leverage your expertise by launching coaching programs, eBooks, or online courses to create cash flow.

11. **Business Income** – Reinvent your revenue model to self-fund growth through consistent monthly income.

Remember, your job is not to fund the vision, it's to lead it. The funding will come when you have a strong plan, a clear purpose, and the right strategy in place. This book is your guide to doing just that.

HOW TO FIND AND WIN RFP (REQUEST FOR PROPOSAL) OPPORTUNITIES

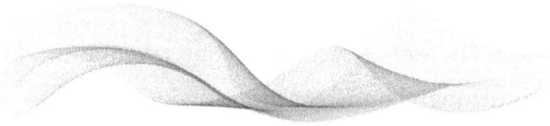

If you're serious about securing consistent, contract-based funding, you must get familiar with RFPs—Request for Proposals. An RFP is a formal document issued by a government agency, corporation, or organization inviting businesses or nonprofits to submit a proposal to complete a specific project or provide a particular service.

In simple terms, an RFP is a company or organization saying, "Here's the work we need done. Tell us how you can do it, what it will cost, and why we should choose you."

WHAT MAKES RFPS A GAME CHANGER?

Unlike many grants, RFPs are contract-based opportunities. That means you're not just getting money, you're securing a client. These contracts can last several months or even years and often include renewal options and consistent payments.

For example, if you run a business that offers training and development services, you could respond to an RFP from your local Department of Labor that's seeking facilitators for youth workforce programs. If your proposal is selected, you're awarded the contract and paid to deliver the training. The more RFPs you win, the more predictable revenue streams you can build into your business or nonprofit.

HOW TO FIND RFP OPPORTUNITIES

Let's move beyond outdated methods and focus on modern, AI-powered strategies that actually save you time and bring better results.

Step 1: Use AI Tools to Automate RFP Discovery

Instead of manually searching every day, you can set up AI-driven alerts and search tools that notify you when new RFPs in your industry or region are posted.

- Use **Google Alerts** with keywords like "Training RFP Tennessee 2025" or "Health and Wellness Service Contract California."
- Leverage AI platforms like **GovWin**, **BidNet**, and **OpenGrants** to track and categorize RFPs based on your business type.
- Use ChatGPT or other AI writing tools to quickly summarize long RFP documents and extract key deadlines, requirements, and evaluation criteria.

Step 2: Conduct Targeted Searches

Spend at least one hour each week (not each day!) refining your search by being specific with your keywords. Examples include:

- RFP youth mentoring programs 2025
- Request for proposal health education services
- Training service provider contract Department of Education
- Community reentry RFP + [your state]

Step 3: Identify 3 to 5 Solid RFPs You Can Win

Once you've gathered a few strong matches, choose 3 to 5 RFPs that align with your business or nonprofit's strengths. Look for ones that match your experience, service offerings, and impact area. You don't need to chase every opportunity, focus on the ones that are the best fit.

Step 4: Create One Strong Proposal Template (Then Customize It)

The biggest mistake people make is starting from scratch every time. Instead, develop one strong master proposal that highlights your business capabilities, team qualifications, past performance, and methodology. Then customize that proposal based on the specific details of each RFP, budget, timeline, outcomes, and submission format.

Step 5: Track Deadlines, Deliverables, and Submission Requirements

Keep in mind that most RFPs follow specific timelines, often aligned with the government fiscal year (October to September). Use tools like Asana https://asana.com/, ClickUp https://clickup.com/, or Notion https://www.notion.com/ to track due dates, submission portals, and follow-up reminders.

Here's a great example, let's say you run a consulting firm that specializes in leadership development and business training. You come across an RFP from your local Department of Economic Development that is looking for certified trainers to deliver workshops to minority-owned startups. Your business aligns perfectly with the project. You submit a proposal detailing your background, experience, and course outline, along with a competitive budget. A few weeks later, you receive the award letter. Not only do you get funding, but you now have a new government client. That's the power of RFPs.

TOP RFP DISCOVERY RESOURCES

Here are several up-to-date resources you can use to discover RFP opportunities:

- **Novae Grants Portal**: https://grants.novaegrants.com
- **F6S Accelerators & Competitions**: https://www.f6s.com/programs
- **GovWin by Deltek** (for government contracts): https://www.deltek.com/en/products/government-contracting/govwin-iq
- **GrantWatch – RFP Section**: https://www.grantwatch.com

Your State or City Procurement Site (search "procurement" + your city or state name)

Examples:

- **Virginia Department of Transportation: http://virginiadot.org/business/rfps.asp**
- **City of Philadelphia: http://www.phila.gov/rfp**
- **California Energy Commission: http://www.energy.ca.gov/contracts/index.html**

If you want consistent income, contract opportunities, and a more sustainable funding strategy, mastering the RFP process is a must. Combine it with AI tools, smart systems, and a winning proposal, and you'll be ready to secure funding that doesn't just support your vision but sustains it for years to come.

CROWDFUNDING RESOURCES

Crowdfunding has become one of the most accessible and effective ways to raise funds for your business or nonprofit. In simple terms, crowdfunding is the process of collecting small amounts of money from a large number of people, usually through online platforms, to fund a project, product, or cause. It's a powerful alternative to traditional financing because it not only brings in money, but also builds a community of supporters around your mission.

Unlike banks or investors that may require credit checks, collateral, or a lengthy approval process, crowdfunding allows you to tell your story, share your vision, and invite people to invest in your success. The best part? You get to raise capital while building awareness, validating your idea, and gaining momentum, all at once.

Here are some of the top crowdfunding platforms that I recommend exploring based on your industry, audience, and funding goals:

1. IFundWomen
https://ifundwomen.com/

A powerful platform specifically for women-led businesses and nonprofits. IFundWomen offers coaching, access to corporate grant opportunities, and a built-in community that believes in the pay-it-forward model. It's more than crowdfunding, it's a movement to close the funding gap for women entrepreneurs.

2. Kickstarter
https://www.kickstarter.com/

One of the most well-known crowdfunding platforms focused on creative and product-based projects. You must hit your funding goal to receive funds, and you'll need to offer rewards to backers. It's a great platform for artists, tech innovators, and makers.

3. Indiegogo
https://www.indiegogo.com/

Unlike Kickstarter, Indiegogo allows you to keep the funds you raise, even if you don't meet your goal. It's flexible, great for startups and social impact initiatives, and integrates well with social media and email marketing.

4. GoFundMe
https://www.gofundme.com/

Though it's often associated with personal causes, GoFundMe can also be used for community-focused business initiatives, nonprofit projects, and small business recovery campaigns. It's simple to set up and trusted by millions.

To truly succeed with crowdfunding, you must go beyond simply launching a campaign, you need a strategy that builds excitement and trust. Start by using AI tools like ChatGPT to help you craft a compelling campaign story. These tools can also assist in writing your FAQs, thank-you messages, and email marketing content that keeps your audience informed and engaged.

Make sure your campaign includes high-quality visuals. Professional photos and videos not only draw attention but also build credibility. People want to see the face behind the mission and understand exactly what they're supporting. Take the time to show your product, service, or impact in action, it can make all the difference.

If the platform allows it, consider offering meaningful incentives or rewards. These don't have to be expensive; even a personalized thank-you or digital download can go a long way. Incentives can encourage more people to contribute and make them feel like they're truly part of your journey.

Before you go live, tap into your existing community. Use your social media audience and email list to generate early momentum. People are more likely to support something that already has traction. Encourage your supporters to share the campaign with their networks to expand your reach.

Once your campaign is live, don't go silent. Stay actively engaged with your backers. Post regular updates, respond to comments, and express gratitude. This level of transparency and communication builds trust and keeps your supporters connected to your progress. Crowdfunding is more than a financial transaction, it's a relationship. The stronger your relationship with your backers, the more likely they'll support you now and in the future.

Crowdfunding isn't just about raising money. It's about inviting your community to be part of your journey. When done right, it can become one of your most powerful tools for building both capital and credibility.

CORPORATE SPONSORSHIPS: HOW TO SECURE BUSINESS PARTNERSHIPS

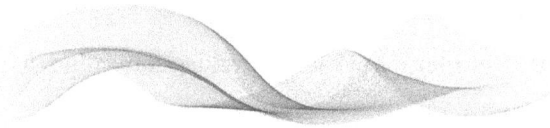

Corporate sponsorship is a partnership between a business or nonprofit and a corporation in which the company provides financial or in-kind support in exchange for brand visibility, community engagement, and alignment with a shared mission or cause. Unlike traditional advertising, corporate sponsorships are typically tied to specific events, programs, or initiatives and are designed to benefit both the sponsor and the sponsored organization.

THE PROS AND CONS OF CORPORATE SPONSORSHIPS

Corporate sponsorships can be a game-changer for small businesses and nonprofits. But like any funding opportunity, they come with their own set of advantages and challenges.

Pros:

- **Access to funding and resources** without taking on debt or giving away equity.

- **Increased visibility and credibility** through association with a known brand.
- **Expanded reach** by tapping into the corporation's audience and marketing channels.
- **Mutual value creation**, both you and the sponsor benefit.

Cons:

- **Requires time and effort** to build relationships and tailor proposals.
- **Brand alignment is critical.** If values don't align, it can hurt your reputation.
- **Reporting obligations** and expectations may require extra coordination.
- **Limited flexibility**, funds are often tied to specific deliverables or visibility commitments.

STEP-BY-STEP PROCESS TO SECURE A CORPORATE SPONSORSHIP

Securing corporate sponsorships doesn't happen overnight. It requires clarity, consistency, and a compelling pitch. When you understand what corporations are looking for, and how to position yourself as a valuable partner, you can open doors to opportunities that provide long-term support and mutual success. The following step-by-step process will walk you through exactly how to identify, approach, and win over corporate sponsors for your business or nonprofit initiative.

Step 1: Identify Aligned Corporations Start by researching companies whose values, mission, and audience align with your business or nonprofit. Look at corporations in your local area, those you already support as a customer, or those with a known track record of giving back.

Step 2: Develop a Sponsorship Package

Create a professional sponsorship proposal that includes:

- A compelling story about your organization and its impact
- Clear sponsorship tiers with benefits for each level
- Details on how the corporation's support will be recognized (e.g., social media mentions, logo placement, speaking opportunities)
- Metrics for measuring success

Step 3: Use AI to Craft and Personalize Your Proposal

Tools like ChatGPT can help you write personalized sponsorship letters, sponsorship deck copy, and email outreach messages. Use AI to help you find keywords that resonate with corporate social responsibility (CSR) goals.

Step 4: Reach Out to the Right Contact

Find the right department typically Community Engagement, corporate social responsibility (CSR), or Marketing and identify a contact person. You can use LinkedIn, the company's website, or networking events to make the connection. Be concise and professional in your initial outreach.

Step 5: Follow Up and Schedule a Discovery Call

Don't stop after sending one email. Follow up a week later and offer to schedule a short call to discuss how a partnership would benefit both parties.

Step 6: Customize the Partnership

Be willing to co-create the sponsorship with the corporation. Some may want brand visibility, others may want to provide volunteers or teach a class. Make it a win-win.

Step 7: Deliver and Report

Once you secure the sponsorship, deliver on everything you promised. Keep your sponsor in the loop with updates, pictures, and outcomes. Send a final impact report at the end that shows the return on their investment.

MY STORY: THE POWER OF SPONSORSHIP

When I first moved to Nashville, TN, I felt a deep calling to give back. I wanted to go into low-income communities and teach Financial Empowerment Workshops. I had personally relied on public assistance at one point in my life, and while I was grateful for the help, I knew I didn't want to stay there. I committed myself to learning everything I could about getting out of debt and building wealth, and I created a system that worked.

I didn't want to keep that success to myself. I wanted to share it. So, I developed a program and pitched it to a local credit union. They said yes. The credit union sponsored the entire workshop. Their sponsorship allowed me to provide marketing, custom workbooks, door prizes, gift cards, gas cards, and food for the participants. But it didn't stop there.

The credit union was invited to attend the workshop and even led a session on financial literacy. They were able to offer second-chance bank accounts to attendees who had previously been denied access to traditional banking services. Everyone won. The sponsor got community exposure and built new customer relationships. I received funding and support to run a high-quality event. And the participants left empowered with tools, resources, and new hope for their financial future.

That experience taught me that corporate sponsorships aren't just about money, they're about impact, collaboration, and transformation.

Now it's your turn.

BUSINESS PLAN COMPETITIONS: A HIDDEN GEM FOR FUNDING AND EXPOSURE

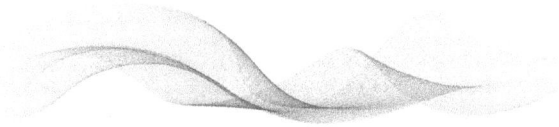

A business plan competition is an organized contest where entrepreneurs pitch their business ideas to a panel of judges, often including investors, business leaders, and grant funders, for a chance to win cash prizes, seed funding, mentorship, or access to valuable business resources. These competitions are a great way to refine your pitch, gain exposure, and validate your idea in a competitive, real-world setting.

Pros:

- Cash prizes and startup funding for winners and finalists
- Access to mentors, investors, and strategic partners
- Feedback to improve your business model
- Increased visibility and credibility in your industry or region

Cons:

- Time-intensive preparation (business plan, pitch deck, practice)
- Highly competitive environment
- Not guaranteed funding. The key is you must stand out among other participants

BUSINESS PLAN COMPETITIONS
YOU SHOULD KNOW ABOUT

Rice Business Plan Competition
https://rbpc.rice.edu/

One of the largest graduate-level competitions in the world, offering over $1 million in prizes. Startups compete in Houston, Texas, and pitch to investors and experts.

MIT $100K Entrepreneurship Competition
https://entrepreneurship.mit.edu/competitions/

Hosted by the Massachusetts Institute of Technology, this competition awards startups across several tracks including pitch, accelerate, and launch. It's a major platform for tech, biotech, and innovation-focused ventures.

Kean Business Plan Competition 2025
https://www.kean.edu/kean-university-business-plan-competition?utm_source=chatgpt.com

This competition offers a platform for aspiring entrepreneurs and small business owners to showcase their innovative ideas. It features two tracks: the "NextGen Innovators Track" for new business concepts and the "Community Roots Track" for existing small businesses. Participants have the opportunity to present their business plans to a panel of experts, receive valuable feedback, and compete for cash prizes.

New York StartUP! 2025 Business Plan Competition
https://www.nypl.org/business/events/new-york-startup-business-plan-competition?utm_source=chatgpt.com

Organized by the New York Public Library, this competition is designed for budding entrepreneurs aiming to launch their businesses. It provides participants with access to library resources, mentorship, and cash prizes ranging from $7,500 to $15,000. The program supports contestants in turning their business ideas into reality.

J. Donald Lee Center for Entrepreneurship Business Plan Competition 2025

https://www.valdosta.edu/colleges/business/deans-office/j.-donald-lee-center-for-entrepreneurship/2025-business-plan-competition.php?utm_source=chatgpt.com

Hosted by Valdosta State University in Georgia, this competition prepares students to start new businesses by developing comprehensive business plans. It emphasizes identifying business opportunities, conducting market research, and developing communication and organizational skills. The competition is open to VSU students and local high school students, encouraging collaboration and practical experience in entrepreneurship.

Whether you're a nonprofit founder or a for-profit entrepreneur, business plan competitions can help you unlock funding, test your pitch, and gain valuable connections. Don't just plan your business, pitch it to win!

PITCH COMPETITIONS: ACE YOUR NEXT OPPORTUNITY

A pitch competition is an event where entrepreneurs present their business ideas to a panel of judges in hopes of winning funding, exposure, mentorship, or valuable business resources. It's one of the fastest-growing ways to get your business noticed and funded. Especially if you know how to prepare and deliver a powerful pitch. These competitions are typically fast-paced, high-energy, and packed with innovation. Your job is to communicate your value, vision, and potential impact with clarity and confidence.

Pros:

- Opportunity to win funding, resources, or partnerships
- Valuable feedback from experts and potential investors
- Increased visibility and credibility for your business
- Network-building with other entrepreneurs and judges

Cons:

- Can be highly competitive
- Time-intensive preparation process
- No guarantee of winning

THE 10-STEP PROCESS TO ACE YOUR NEXT PITCH COMPETITION:

Step 1: Understand the Rules – Read every detail. Know the presentation format, time limit, and judging criteria.

Step 2: Define Your Value Proposition – Clearly explain what makes your business unique and how it solves a problem.

Step 3: Know Your Audience – Research the judges and tailor your message to resonate with their background and priorities.

Step 4: Craft a Compelling Story – Create a narrative that includes the problem, your solution, your journey, and your mission.

Step 5: Prepare Your Pitch Deck – Keep it clear, visual, and focused. Highlight your product, market size, traction, financials, and team.

Step 6: Practice Your Delivery – Rehearse until your pitch feels natural. Use confident body language and control your pacing.

Step 7: Anticipate Questions – Prepare answers for common concerns like competition, scalability, and financial sustainability.

Step 8: Gather Feedback – Present to mentors and revise your pitch based on their input.

Step 9: Perfect Your Executive Summary – Bring a one-page overview of your business for judges and investors.

Step 10: Stay Calm and Confident – Believe in your vision and let your passion shine.

My Favorite Tip: Use AI tools to fine-tune your script, generate sample questions, and improve your pitch deck design.

PITCH COMPETITIONS YOU SHOULD APPLY FOR:

NAACP Powershift Entrepreneur Pitch Competition
https://naacp.org

Launched by the NAACP and Daymond John, this competition targets Black entrepreneurs and provides funding and mentorship.

She Loves Tech Global Startup Competition
https://www.shelovestech.org/

Focused on women-led and tech-based startups, this competition connects winners with global investors and accelerator programs.

Stacy's Rise Project Pitch Competition
https://www.stacysrise.com/

Supported by PepsiCo, this program provides funding and mentorship for female entrepreneurs in the food and beverage industry.

Calling All North Alabama Entrepreneurs: Enter to Win $25,000 Pitch Competition
https://launchtnvalley.org/entrepreneurship/launch-tank/

The Singing River Trail Launch Tank is here to give North Alabama entrepreneurs the chance to pitch their ideas for up to $25,000 in cash and prizes! Whether you're just starting out or looking to scale, this competition is the perfect opportunity to gain exposure, connect with business leaders, and get the support you need. Think Shark Tank- but local!

HatchThis 2025 Pitch Competition Up to $20,000

https://hatchinnovationhub.org/event/hatch-this-2025/

Back after a pandemic break, for the fourth year, HatchThis brings a game-changing mash-up of an accelerator, a hackathon, and a weekend-long party for the Asheville entrepreneurial community. HatchThis offers a unique combination of world-class business acumen and startup intensity – all designed to help participants compete for $20,000 in prizes, including a $5,000 cash seed funding package.

Pitch Perfect Grant $5,000 Grant

https://helloskip.com/dashboard/opportunity/pitchperfect2

The Pitch Perfect Grant, a collaboration between Pink Print, Ellie Talks Money, and Skip, is offering a $5,000 grant to help entrepreneurs expand their businesses.

America's Seed Fund Project Pitch - For Small Businesses

https://seedfund.nsf.gov/apply/project-pitch/

This opportunity helps startups navigate the earliest stages of technology translation. Each startup can receive up to $2 million to support translational research and development. From advanced manufacturing to artificial intelligence to biological technologies to environmental technologies, they fund nearly all areas of technology.

Spring 2025 Agora Venture Competition

https://www.theagorainitiative.com/venture-competition

The Spring 2025 Agora Venture Competition offers an exciting platform for startups to pitch their business ideas to some of Washington, D.C.'s most influential investors. With a $10,000 cash prize and unmatched exposure, this competition is perfect for trailblazers and disruptors ready to scale their ventures. If you're a startup founder with a bold vision and a strong pitch, this is your opportunity to elevate your business to new heights.

Whether you're a seasoned speaker or brand new to pitching, the best way to win is to show up prepared, passionate, and polished. Don't just aim to pitch, aim to win.

CHAPTER 5

GRANT FUNDING OPPORTUNITIES & RESOURCES

GRANTS FOR WOMEN-OWNED BUSINESSES

CÎROC's Blue Dot Creative Residency – Amount: up to $500,000

https://www.ciroc.com/en-us/bluedotresidency

The Blue Dot Creative Residency, created in partnership with MACRO, provides funding to empower creatives in fashion, art, music, and entertainment to develop a passion project in a new creative vertical. This inaugural grant initiative awards up to $500,000 to eliminate barriers and support visionary creatives with capital and resources.

Caltech Rocket Fund – Amount: $25,000 - $100,000

https://rocketfund.caltech.edu/about-us

The Rocket Fund offers non-equity grants of $25,000 to $100,000 to cleantech and sustainability startups across the U.S. Recipients gain access to partnerships with major corporations and technical resources, enhancing commercialization and scale-up potential.

Catalyst CTIA Wireless Foundation

https://www.wirelessfoundation.org/catalyst

The Catalyst program supports early-stage social entrepreneurs who are developing mobile-first solutions powered by wireless technology to create social impact. Up to six applicants will receive unrestricted grants, including a $100,000 first-place prize, along with non-financial support to scale their innovations.

Cartier Women's Initiative
https://www.cartierwomensinitiative.com/about

The Cartier Women's Initiative awards funding and a year-long fellowship to female entrepreneurs making a social or environmental impact through innovative business solutions. Grants are awarded across three categories, Regional, Science & Technology Pioneer, and Diversity, Equity & Inclusion, supporting global impact and access.

Ulta's MUSE Accelerator
https://www.ulta.com/company/dei/muse/muse-accelerator

Ulta's MUSE Accelerator provides $50,000 grants to eight BIPOC beauty brand founders and offers a 10-week program focused on retail readiness, mentorship, and industry support. The program is designed to drive long-term success through financial investment and business development resources.

Beyond Open
https://www.beyondopenclt.com/

Beyond Open is a small business grant program focused on building economic mobility for diverse-owned businesses in Charlotte's Corridors of Opportunity. Supported by Wells Fargo, the initiative has awarded $16.3 million to 402 local businesses since 2022.

Fifteen Percent Pledge Achievement Award
https://15percentpledge.org/award/achievement

The Fifteen Percent Pledge Achievement Award offers $250,000 in total grant funding to three Black-owned businesses, including mentorship and consulting support. Created to address funding disparities, this award helps businesses reach new levels of growth and visibility.

Sephora's Beauty Grant

https://15percentpledge.org/award/sephora

The Sephora Beauty Grant awards one Black beauty entrepreneur a $100,000 grant to support business growth and brand development. Eligible applicants must be part of the Fifteen Percent Pledge Business Equity Community with at least $100K in annual revenue.

She's Connected by AT&T Program

https://www.att.com/shesconnected/

She's Connected by AT&T supports women entrepreneurs and athletes through a grant contest awarding $50,000, a year of AT&T service, and promotional opportunities. Launched in 2020, the program has distributed $90,000 to women-owned businesses.

FedEx Small Business Grant

https://www.fedex.com/en-us/small-business/grants.html

The FedEx Small Business Grant Program awards U.S. entrepreneurs with funding to grow their businesses, including $50,000 for the top recipient and $20,000 for others. Since 2012, the program has distributed over $2 million to more than 120 small businesses nationwide.

Fund Her Future by H&R Block

https://www.blockadvisors.com/fund-her-future-small-business-grants/

Fund Her Future offers over $100,000 in grants and services to five women-owned businesses, with a $50,000 grand prize. Winners also receive one year of expert business services, including bookkeeping, tax support, and compliance consulting.

UpGreyed Her 2025

https://grey.co/iwd25

This opportunity is a financial inclusion initiative by Grey designed to empower female entrepreneurs by providing them with the necessary capital to expand their businesses.

Amber Grant

https://ambergrantsforwomen.com/get-an-amber-grant/

WomensNet founded the Amber Grant Foundation in 1998. The Foundation was set up with one goal in mind: to honor the memory of a very special young woman, Amber Wigdahl, who died at just 19 years old, before realizing her business dreams. Today, WomensNet carries on that tradition, giving away at least $10,000 every month in Amber Grant money. They also expanded our grant-giving to include a year-end grant of $25,000.

The Big Idea Grant

https://www.yippitydoo.com/small-business-grant-optin/

This opportunity was born from a passion to support and uplift women entrepreneurs who are eager to turn their dreams into thriving businesses. From its inception, the goal has been to provide financial resources, mentorship, and guidance, empowering women to succeed. Each month, one recipient is awarded $1,000 to invest in their business and exclusive access to a wealth mindset coaching group to support their growth. Receive mentorship, financial support, and resources tailored to your business goals immediately after being selected.

BIPOC Fitness Grant

https://www.movemeantfoundation.com/bipoc-fitness

At Movemeant Foundation, we believe that every girl has the power within her to achieve greatness. By helping girls believe in themselves both physically and mentally, we are creating a world where girls and women are unstoppable. They award grants to a variety of young female athletes, from economically-disadvantaged communities with high incidences of health-risk behaviors to up-and-coming all-stars who require additional resources for mental, physical and emotional coaching.

EmpowerHer Grant - Boundless Futures Foundation
https://boundlessfutures.org/our-impact/

The Boundless Futures Foundation awards grants to U.S.-based female entrepreneurs and nonprofits that support female entrepreneurship. The EmpowHer Grant offers entrepreneurs up to $25,000, with funds provided as reimbursements for business expenses upon proof of payment. Nonprofits that support female entrepreneurs through education, mentorship, or financing can request up to $30,000 in grant funding through the Her Village Grant.

Entreprenista Evolve Grant - $2,500
https://helloskip.com/dashboard/opportunity/entreprenistaevolve

Are you a woman entrepreneur looking for funding to grow your business? The Evolve Grant is here to support you! This grant is designed to empower founders, amplify their impact, and accelerate their business growth.

HerRise MicroGrant $1,000
https://www.hersuitespot.com/herrise

The 2022 HerRise MicroGrant exists to provide financial aid to women of color that are often unable to secure funding for their small business. Each month a $1,000 microgrant will be awarded to a small business owned by women of color.

Mom Deserves A Time Out

https://thesupermom.org/

The "Mom Deserves A Time Out" grant is here to celebrate one extraordinary mother with a $20,000 prize, a feature in Woman's World Magazine, and an unforgettable luxury getaway for two in Napa, California! If you're a hardworking mom who deserves a much-needed break, this is your moment! Or if you know an extraordinary mom who has gone above and beyond, nominate her today.

The Peanut Grant

https://www.peanut-app.io/starther

StartHER challenges the biases in venture capital and provides access to the elusive 'friends and family' round. For many founders, raising money from friends and family isn't an option because their existing networks don't have resources to offer such funds. StartHER aims to give everyone a fair chance by re-shaping funding dynamics, providing access to professional networks and ultimately, becoming home to the new faces of entrepreneurship.

RTC Women in Tech Fund. Rewriting The Code (RTC)

https://rewritingthecode.org/women-in-tech-fund/

Rewriting the Code's mission is to disrupt gender and racial inequity in the tech industry by equipping and empowering college and early career women in tech. To advance this mission, they are proud to offer the RTC Women in Tech Fund, a financial resource aimed at propelling their student members past urgent financial obstacles to completing their degrees.

Makers Mindset Workshop & Grant

https://makersmindset.com/workshop/

Led by beauty industry powerhouse Nancy Twine, this immersive crash course and grant is designed for early-stage female entrepreneurs in the CPG (consumer packaged goods) space. Whether you're in beauty, food, beverage, pet, tech goods, or home goods, this is your chance to grow with expert guidance.

Olga Loizon Memorial Foundation

https://www.olgas.com/foundation/

The Olga Loizon Memorial Foundation offers grants of up to $10,000 to aspiring women entrepreneurs in Michigan who embody the passion and vision of Olga Loizon, the founder of metro Detroit's Olga's Kitchen.

GRANTS FOR MINORITY ENTREPRENEURS

Santander
https://app.santanderx.com/calls/csb12

The Cultivate Small Business Cohort 12 offers $20,000 in grant funding and a 12-week program designed for early-stage food industry entrepreneurs, with a focus on supporting women, immigrant, and BIPOC-owned businesses in low-to-moderate income neighborhoods.

Bakersfield Entrepreneurship Ecosystem Technical Assistance and Grant Program
https://www.bakersfieldcity.us/1108/Entrepreneurship-Grant-Program

This program supports minority-owned businesses in Bakersfield, California, with technical assistance and grants up to $40,000. It focuses on helping entrepreneurs overcome financial and operational barriers to growth, with an emphasis on fostering economic equity in underrepresented communities.

The Breva Thrive Grant

https://www.breva.ai/thrive-grant?utm_source=substack&utm_medium=email

A quarterly $5,000 grant designed to support entrepreneurs who are creating jobs, innovating products, or making services more accessible.

Galaxy Grants

https://galaxyofstars.org/galaxy-grants/

Galaxy Grants is on a mission to support women and minority entrepreneurs with their small businesses by offering valuable resources, tools, funding, and knowledge. They are running a $2,450 Galaxy Grant Giveaway, sponsored by Hidden Star, a 501(c)(3) organization, with a quick 30-second entry process. Plus, there's an opportunity to win for both you and a friend, as each of you could receive a $2,450 grant if your friend wins, subject to the Terms and Conditions.

Friends & Family Fund

https://www.skysthelimit.org/friends-family-fund

Awards monthly grants of up to $2,500 to young entrepreneurs (ages 18–30) from underrepresented backgrounds. The fund prioritizes founders who lack traditional access to capital and provides mentorship to help them scale early-stage ventures.

Juntos Crecemos Hispanic Digital & Delivery Program (PepsiCo)

https://pepsicojuntoscrecemos.com/jefaowned/

Designed for Latina entrepreneurs in the food service industry, this program offers 8 weeks of mentorship on digital tools, marketing, and operations. Participants gain resources to enhance their online presence and compete in the digital economy.

Just Thrive $6,000 Grant Program

https://lively-sky-489.myflodesk.com/y23xj979kc

Provides $6,000 in HR and payroll support to businesses with at least 50% ownership by underrepresented groups. The grant targets systemic inequities by helping entrepreneurs invest in essential infrastructure and workforce development.

Kickass Single Mom Stimulus Grant

https://www.wealthysinglemommy.com/single-mom-grant/

Every month, they give out $500 cash to one single mom, no strings attached. The Kickass Single Mom Stimulus Grant has one goal: Give a hand to single moms struggling with money, health, stress, childcare, illness and loneliness.

Kinetic Black Business Support Fund

https://business.windstream.com/bbsf

Offers grants to Black-owned small businesses in Georgia, North Carolina, or Kentucky using Windstream broadband services. Funding is awarded first-come, first-served to help businesses improve operations, marketing, or tech infrastructure.

The Kitty Fund Mother-Led Business Grant

https://foundersfirstcdc.org/kitty-fund

Calling all Mompreneurs! This is your chance to get the support you deserve. The Grant Amount is $25,000 to 25 Mompreneurs nationwide. In order to apply you must be a U.S.-based mothers with businesses (2-100 employees, revenue under $5M).

Minority Business Circle
https://minoritybusinesscircle.com/

A membership platform providing grants, loans, and discounts on business tools for minority-owned ventures. Members access a step-by-step growth guide, mentorship, and tailored resources to accelerate their businesses.

MSP Equity Accelerator sponsored by Allianz
https://www.gener8tor.com/investment-accelerators/msp-equity-accelerator

The MSP Equity Accelerator sponsored by Allianz invests in high-growth startups founded by Black, Brown and Women entrepreneurs. For each cohort, $100K is invested in each of five startups who receive a concierge experience during our 12-week accelerator program. Founders must be willing to travel to Minnesota for In-Person Components of the program.

Small Certified Supplier Innovative Finance Program
https://foundersfirstcapitalpartners.com/small-certified-supplier-innovative-finance-program/

Awards $5,000 grants to certified diverse suppliers in California, Georgia, and other states. The program includes financial training and matches businesses with investors to build capacity and secure long-term funding.

Tidal Empowerment Program
https://empowerment.tidalcommerce.ca/

Partners with Shopify to offer minority-led businesses $25,000 in consulting (strategy, marketing, tech) and a tech bundle. The program focuses on closing the digital divide for underrepresented entrepreneurs.

Wish Local up to $2,000 Grant

https://www.wish.com/local/empowerment

Awards $500–$2,000 to Black-owned small businesses as part of Wish's $2M equity initiative. Grants help businesses recover from systemic challenges and expand their e-commerce presence on the Wish platform.

The Famous Amos Ingredients for Success (IFS) Entrepreneurs Initiative - For Black Business Owners

https://famousamosingredientsforsuccess.com/

This opportunity creates pathways for early-stage Black business owners to thrive by providing $150,000 in capital awards, mentorship, networking, and educational resources. Honoring Wally Amos' legacy and the "Famously You" ethos, this initiative celebrates the qualities that make each business owner unique and fosters long-term success for their businesses.

GRANTS FOR STARTUPS & SMALL BUSINESSES

America's Seed Fund Project Pitch

https://seedfund.nsf.gov/apply/project-pitch/

This opportunity helps startups navigate the earliest stages of technology translation. Each startup can receive up to $2 million to support translational research and development. From advanced manufacturing to artificial intelligence to biological technologies to environmental technologies, they fund nearly all areas of technology.

The Breakthrough $10,000 Grant

https://www.honeycombcredit.com/breakthrough

Make 2025 your breakthrough year! The start of a new year brings endless possibilities, and this grant is designed to help small business owners like you, visionaries ready to take their dreams to the next level.

The Freed Fellowship $2,500 Grant

https://www.freedfellowship.com/grant1

Awards monthly grants to small businesses with social impact goals. Recipients also receive mentorship, feedback, and access to a community of entrepreneurs to refine their business models.

Hustler's MicroGrant
https://www.hersuitespot.com/hustlersgrant/

Provides $1,000 monthly grants to U.S. small businesses, prioritizing underrepresented founders. The program emphasizes quick, no-strings-attached funding to help entrepreneurs scale operations or launch new products.

The Breva Thrive Grant - For Small Businesses
https://www.breva.ai/thrive-grant

Small businesses keep our communities alive and vibrant. Every quarter, a $5,000 grant is awarded to an entrepreneur who positively impacts an underrepresented community. Your business must have a demonstrated impact on its community, such as creating new jobs, innovating new products, or making products and services more accessible. Breva strongly prefers businesses operating for at least 1 year and generating a minimum annual revenue of $35,000.

ICECA Fast Track Grant Program
https://www.iron.org/fast-track-grant

Offers up to $2,500 to startups in Iron County, Utah, to attract new businesses to the area. Grants are awarded based on innovation, job creation, and community impact.

The Michael & Susan Dell Foundation
https://www.dell.org/

The Michael & Susan Dell Foundation provides grants exceeding $50,000 to for-profit and nonprofit social enterprises that directly impact education, health, and family economic stability for children and youth.

Miller Center for Social Entrepreneurship

https://www.millersocent.org/accelerator/

Must be a social enterprise that is intentional about supporting women's economic empowerment, climate resilience, or the intersection of both and have at least $50K in income.

Visa's Everywhere Initiative

https://usa.visa.com/visa-everywhere/everywhere-initiative/initiative.html

This is a series of three challenges meant to test start-up's ingenuity, creativity, and innovative commerce ideas. Last year, Visa selected 600 start-ups to compete in the challenges, which awarded the winners up to $50,000 each. Check out their website for more information.

Bakersfield Entrepreneurship Ecosystem Technical Assistance and up to $40K Grant

https://www.bakersfieldcity.us/1108/Entrepreneurship-Grant-Program

The City of Bakersfield Entrepreneurship Ecosystem Technical Assistance and Grant Program is a visionary initiative aimed at providing crucial support to local minority-based businesses in need.

National Association for the Self-Employed Growth Grants

https://www.nase.org/become-a-member/member-benefits/business-resources/growth-grants

Awards up to $4,000 to self-employed individuals and small businesses. Applicants must be NASE members and submit a detailed plan for using funds to drive growth.

Substack Creator Accelerator Fund

https://read.substack.com/p/substack-creator-accelerator-fund

Provides funding and mentorship to U.S.-based creators with at least $2,000 in monthly revenue. The program helps writers, podcasters, and artists grow their subscription-based audiences.

Z Fellows $10,000 Grant

https://www.zfellows.com/

Awards $10,000 to early-stage tech founders working on projects in AI, climate tech, biotech, or hardware. Recipients join a cohort for mentorship and pitch opportunities.

Another Chance for Businesses Grant

https://www.anotherchanceforsmallbusinesses.org/grant

This quarterly grant program is built to support startups and small businesses facing hardship. If you need a boost to get back on track, here's your opportunity to receive the support you deserve.

The Well Work

https://docs.google.com/forms/d/e/1FAIpQLSfBliPqGUpF_4XAyam7ddCzZaOP4OqB6jq5ZEGjtHFgRAQUxw/viewform?pli=1

The Just Thrive Program offers up to $6,000 in funding to existing businesses that are at least 50% owned by marginalized founders and have a minimum of two W-2 employees.

776 Fellowship

https://776.org/

A $100K in grant funding to young builders aged 18-24 who are creating measurable solutions that will benefit underserved communities.

Camelback Fellowship

https://www.camelbackventures.org/apply/

This opportunity provides $40,000 in grant funding or SAFE notes, along with a 16-week Fellowship program for early-stage entrepreneurs committed to addressing inequities in the education and technology sectors.

GRANTS FOR NONPROFITS & COMMUNITY-BASED ORGANIZATIONS

Believe in Reading Grants

https://believeinreading.org/grant-guidelines/

This opportunity will consider funding programs that serve any age or aspect of supporting reading and literacy, including adult literacy or English as a second language projects. The funder's favorite things to help applicants purchase are books and materials, especially for building libraries or using grant funds to stock a book vending machine but not purchasing the machine itself. Awards range from $1,000 to $10,000.

The Buster Coleman Charitable Trust $25,000 Grant

https://www.wellsfargo.com/private-foundations/coleman-foundation/

The Buster Coleman Charitable Trust provide grant funding up to $25,000 to support religious, charitable, scientific, literary or educational purposes and the prevention of cruelty to children or animals.

Chick-fil-A's True Inspiration Awards®

https://www.chick-fil-a.com/true-inspiration-awards/learn-more

Imagine what your nonprofit could achieve with up to $350,000 in grant funding! More programs, greater impact, and stronger communities, this is your moment to step forward and secure the funding your organization deserves!

The Christopher D. Smithers Foundation

https://smithersfoundation.org/

Awards up to $25,000 to nonprofits combating alcoholism stigma, especially in high-risk populations like youth and minority communities. Grants support prevention programs and public education campaigns.

Cisco Global Impact Cash Grants

https://www.cisco.com/c/en/us/about/csr/community/nonprofits/global-impact-cash-grants.html

Supports nonprofits using technology to amplify social impact. Grants prioritize projects with scalable solutions in education, healthcare, or economic empowerment.

Costco $5,000 Grant

https://www.costco.com/charitable-giving.html

Funds nonprofits focused on children, education, and health in communities where Costco operates. Applications are reviewed quarterly, with a focus on measurable outcomes.

DanPaul Foundation Grants

https://www.danpaulfoundation.org/grant-funding-guidelines

Provides up to $15,000 to youth-focused nonprofits for education, health, and environmental programs. The foundation prioritizes direct service over administrative costs.

The Foundation for Financial Planning $40,000 Grant

https://ffpprobono.org/our-work/grants/

Nonprofits that engage CFP® professionals as volunteers to provide free, one-on-one financial planning to underserved individuals (veterans, cancer patients, seniors, low-income families).

The John Templeton Foundation $230,000 Grant

https://www.templeton.org/grants/apply-for-grant

The John Templeton Foundation provides grant opportunities to non-profit organizations of up to $230,000 to support education, research, and outreach projects that promote individual freedom, free markets, free competition, and entrepreneurship.

Literacy Opportunity $6,000 Grant Fund

https://www.proliteracy.org/grants-funding/literacy-opportunity-fund/

Grants through our Literacy Opportunity Fund help US-based nonprofit organizations do their work in transforming lives through adult literacy. They award grants up to $6,000 to literacy organizations of all types and sizes that are doing direct work with adult students. Apply for a grant to fund your organization's general operating expenses, such as salaries or teacher stipends, supplies or equipment, space rental, and more. Or, apply for a Literacy Opportunity award to fund a particular project, event, or new programming development.

The Michael & Susan Dell Foundation
https://www.dell.org/

The Michael & Susan Dell Foundation provides grants exceeding $50,000 to for-profit and nonprofit social enterprises that directly impact education, health, and family economic stability for children and youth.

The Pollination Project
https://thepollinationproject.org/apply/

Offers $1,000–$40,000 to grassroots nonprofits globally for projects promoting kindness, justice, or sustainability. Applicants must have an annual budget under $50,000.

Salesforce Power of Us Program
https://www.salesforce.org/power-of-us/

Provides free or discounted Salesforce software to nonprofits. Organizations also gain access to training and resources to optimize donor management and outreach.

The Vilcek Foundation Grant
https://vilcek.org/grants/

The Vilcek Foundation provides funding to nonprofit organizations that champion the contributions of immigrants in the arts, sciences, and humanities. This grant is designed to uplift and amplify immigrant voices by supporting initiatives that foster diversity, equity, and inclusion. If your nonprofit organization is actively involved in promoting cultural understanding and empowering immigrant creatives, this grant opportunity is for you.

TD Charitable Foundation Grants up to $150,000

https://www.td.com/us/en/about-us/communities/ready-commitment/funding-opportunities/non-profit

The TD Charitable Foundation's Capacity Building Fund provides grants to nonprofit organizations in TD Bank's U.S. market areas for training, talent, tools, and tactics to further help their programs succeed. The Fund includes two opportunities: Capacity Building Grants provide funding to help strengthen and increase the impact of organizations on the communities they serve. These grants support work around three key issues: tactics, talent, and tools. The Nonprofit Training Resource Fund supports specific trainings that increase the capacities and skill sets of organizations' employees. For both opportunities, support is primarily provided for programs aligned to one of TD's corporate citizenship priorities: better health, connected communities, financial security, and a vibrant planet. Applicants must have annual operating budgets of $2 million or less and serve low- to moderate-income communities and diverse or historically underserved communities. Eligible areas are CT, DE, DC, FL, MA, MD, ME, NC, NH, NJ, NY, PA, RI, SC, VA, and VT. Funding up to $150,000.

NBCUniversal Local

https://www.localimpactgrants.com/

$2.5 Million Grant Fund for non-profits in the youth education and empowerment, next-generation storytellers and community engagement sectors.

Waste Management Strategic Innovation Grant

https://www.wm.com/us/en/inside-wm/social-impact/community-impact

Offers grants of up to $150,000 for programs advancing environmental stewardship, sustainability education, workforce development, community vitality, or supplier diversity. Funds are awarded on a rolling basis, apply ASAP, as availability is limited.

GRANTS FOR VETERAN-OWNED BUSINESSES

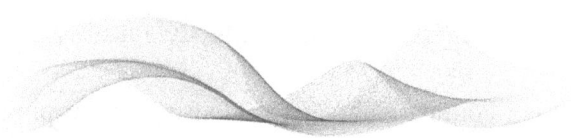

The DAV Charitable Service Trust
https://cst.dav.org/grants/

The DAV Charitable Service Trust is offering grants to support sick, injured, and homeless Veterans by funding:

- Transportation to VA facilities
- Medical aid and rehabilitation
- Essential services for Veterans and their families

With a median grant amount of $30,000 and a focus on long-term assistance programs, this funding can be a game-changer for organizations dedicated to serving those who served us.

Have questions or need assistance? Contact the DAV Charitable Service Trust team: Email: cst@dav.org
Phone: (859) 441-7300, ext. 3309 or 3313

Military Entrepreneur Challenge
https://secondservicefoundation.org/mec/

Offers grants and mentorship to veteran, military spouse, and Gold Star Family entrepreneurs. Participants compete in pitch events for capital to grow their businesses.

Home Depot Foundation's Veteran Housing up to $500,000 Grants Program
https://corporate.homedepot.com/page/veteran-housing-grants

The Home Depot Foundation's Veteran Housing Grants program awards grants to nonprofit organizations for the new construction or rehabilitation of multifamily, permanent supportive housing for veterans throughout the United States, including Puerto Rico. The grants fund physical construction costs, and must comprise less than 50% of the total development cost of the project. While rural areas will be considered, priority will be given to large cities with populations of over 300,000 people.

Bridge The Gap Veterans' Services Grant Program
https://city-of-boston.wizehive.app/program/bridge-the-gap/info?utm_source=Intergovernmental+Relations&utm_campaign=Funding+Update+September+5%2C+2024&utm_medium=email

This opportunity will award mini-grants to organizations that support Boston's veteran community and "Bridge the Gap," which exists after the possible allocation of federal or state benefits. Funds will be used to implement projects and programs that support, honor, recognize, and improve the overall quality of life of the City of Boston veterans, the military community, and their families. Focus areas include Housing, Transportation, Health and Wellness, Upward Economic Mobility, Legal Services, and Educational/Historical Programming. Up to $9,999 will be awarded.

American-Made Heroes Foundation Fund

https://american-madeheroes.com/

Provides annual grants ranging from $4,000 to $6,000 to eligible 501(c)(3) and 501(c)(19) nonprofits that serve the veteran community.

Small Business Technology Transfer (STTR) Grant

https://www.sbir.gov/

Encourages small businesses, including veteran-owned ones, to engage in federal research and development with potential for commercialization.

Veteran Women Igniting the Spirit of Entrepreneurship (V-WISE)

https://ivmf.syracuse.edu/programs/entrepreneurship/start-up/v-wise/

A two-part program offering a 4-week online course on fundamental business skills, followed by a three-day in-person capstone conference, designed for women veterans and female military spouses/partners. (Resource)

The Roux Institute Founder Residency Program

https://roux.northeastern.edu/entrepreneurship/founder-residency/

A year-long accelerator for early-stage tech startups, focusing on supporting underrepresented founders, including veterans; offers $25,000 in non-dilutive funding and extensive resources.

StreetShares Foundation Veteran Small Business Award

https://secondservicefoundation.org/

Provides grants ranging from $4,000 to $15,000 to veteran-owned small businesses, aiming to boost veteran entrepreneurship by offering access to capital.

Entrepreneurship Bootcamp for Veterans (EBV)
http://ebv.vets.syr.edu/

Offers cutting-edge, experiential training in entrepreneurship and small business management to post-9/11 veterans with service-connected disabilities. (Resource)

Hivers & Strivers Capital
https://hiversandstrivers.com/

An angel investment group that invests exclusively in early-stage, highly scalable startups led by U.S. military veterans.

GRANTS FOR HEALTHCARE & WELLNESS INITIATIVES

HRSA Health and Public Safety Workforce Resiliency Grants

https://www.hrsa.gov/grants

The Health Resources and Services Administration (HRSA) funds initiatives that support mental health and wellness among the health workforce. These grants focus on reducing burnout, building resilience, and promoting overall well-being in healthcare settings.

SAMHSA – Mental Health Awareness Training Grants

https://www.samhsa.gov/grants

SAMHSA offers funding to support training and awareness programs for mental health in community and school settings. Programs that include partnerships with first responders and healthcare providers are prioritized.

Movemeant's Meant To Move Grant

https://www.movemeantfoundation.com/grants

Awards $1,000 to young female athletes (ages 8–16) from underserved communities. Funds help cover costs for sports programs, coaching, and wellness resources.

CVS Health Foundation – Health in Action Grants

https://www.cvshealth.com/impact/healthy-community/our-giving/foundations/grants.html

The CVS Health Foundation provides funding for innovative healthcare models and wellness initiatives that improve access to quality care, especially in underserved communities. Grants typically support programs focused on chronic disease management, health equity, and health literacy.

Kaiser Permanente Community Health Grants

https://about.kaiserpermanente.org/commitments-and-impact/healthy-communities/communities-we-serve/northwest-community/our-impact/grants-and-sponsorships

These grants support nonprofit organizations addressing key community health issues such as mental health, food insecurity, and access to care. The initiative prioritizes programs that reduce health disparities and improve community well-being.

The Aetna Foundation – Building Healthy Communities Grant

https://www.thegrantplantnm.com/grant-detail/aetna-foundation-cultivating-healthy-communities-2/

Aetna Foundation grants are awarded to projects that enhance local health outcomes through nutrition education, active living, and health system innovation. The focus is on scalable solutions that make measurable impact in low-income or underserved areas.

Robert Wood Johnson Foundation – Evidence for Action: Innovative Research to Advance Racial Equity

https://www.rwjf.org/en/grants.html

While focused on health equity, this grant supports health and wellness research initiatives that close the gap in racial disparities in healthcare. Projects can include wellness programs, community health innovations, and health system reform.

GRANTS FOR ARTS & CREATIVE ENTERPRISES

The Vimeo Short Film Grant - For Emerging Filmmakers
https://vimeo.com/shortfilmgrant

This opportunity is intended for emerging filmmakers who have completed at least two short films but have yet to complete a feature film. Five $30,000 grants will be awarded for producing an original short film. Applicants will have access to Nikon and RED cameras, training, one-on-one mentorship sessions with celebrated filmmakers, the release on Vimeo. com, and screenings with live audiences.

AMAKA Grants
https://helloskip.com/sign-in?ref=RENEE145

AMAKA Grants offers funding to selected creators, creative freelancers, and creative businesses. It's your opportunity to access top-tier resources and elevate your projects to the next level. Two winners selected monthly and will receive $500 to cover creative software expenses and a free consultation session. Here's how this program works:

The Awesome Foundation $1,000 Grants

https://www.awesomefoundation.org/en

The Awesome Foundation is offering $1,000 grants to help fund programs, projects and ideas that are "awesome". The grants have "no strings", or stipulations. Individuals, nonprofits and for-profits are welcome to apply.

The Recording Fund Grant

https://www.recordingfund.org/apply

Supports independent musicians and artists with funding for studio time and production costs. Grants help artists overcome financial barriers to recording their work.

O'Shaughnessy Fellowships & $100,000 Grants

https://www.osv.llc/oshaughnessy-fellowships

A one-year program that unites the world's most bold and undiscovered researchers, builders and creatives to find, build and spread new ideas.

Calling all Creatives: $20K Grants

https://app.helloalice.com/grants/remy-martin-this-is-my-city-grant/apply

Are you an emerging creative making a notable cultural impact in Atlanta, Chicago, Detroit, or New York City? Rémy Martin's This is My City grant program is seeking visionary artists, musicians, designers, and entrepreneurs who are making an impact in their communities through creative innovation. Four groundbreaking local leaders will each receive a $20K grant, paired with one-on-one mentorship from industry leaders, to amplify their community impact. Whether you're a DJ building bridges through sound, an artist reimagining public spaces, or a cultural entrepreneur mentoring the next generation through arts, this grant aims to help turn your vision into reality.

The Harpo Foundation Grants for Visual Artists

https://www.harpofoundation.org/grants/grants-for-visual-artists/

This award directly supports under-recognized visual artists 21 years old or older to support their development. Funding up to $10,000 will be provided.

Etsy Disaster Relief Fund

https://advocacy.etsy.com/etsy-emergency-relief-fund-at-cerf/

Provides $2,000 quarterly grants to Etsy sellers affected by federally declared disasters. Applicants must have an active shop for at least one year.

WORTHLESSSTUDIOS Photographer in Residence Program

https://www.worthlessstudios.org/photographer-in-residence

Offers a $1,500 stipend and access to a mobile darkroom for emerging photographers. The residency supports artists creating new bodies of work within 3 hours of Brooklyn, NY.

National Geographic's Freshwater Storytelling Grant - For Filmmakers, Photographers & Writers

https://www.nationalgeographic.org/society/grants-and-investments/rfp-freshwater/

This opportunity seeks submissions from storytellers interested in creating and disseminating content that raises public awareness and engagement of critical issues around the sustainable use of freshwater resources. A variety of content formats, including, but not limited to, Photography, Film and Video, Mapmaking, Data Visualization, Written Word, Spoken Word, etc. will be considered. Projects that dig deeper into the challenges facing specific communities, such as last mile households, low-income households, women and girls, and children, in achieving equitable access to freshwater and how these issues are worsening as freshwater scarcity increases are encouraged. Applications are encouraged for projects highlighting specific solutions to these challenges, and elevate the voices of individuals, organizations, and communities at the forefront. Funding ranges from $20,000 to $100,000.

The State of the Art Prize - For Artists
https://creative-capital.org/about-the-creative-capital-award/?mc_cid=73142525d4&mc_eid=45394a798e

This opportunity aims to recognize and support one artist from every U.S. state and inhabited territory with an unrestricted $10,000 artist grant.

The 2025 Whiting Creative Nonfiction Grant
https://www.whiting.org/writers/creative-nonfiction-grant/about

This $40,000 opportunity will be awarded to as many as ten writers who are completing a book-length work of deeply researched and imaginatively composed nonfiction for a general adult readership. It is intended for multiyear book projects requiring large amounts of deep and focused research, thinking, and writing at a crucial point mid-process, after significant work has been accomplished but when an extra infusion of support can make a difference in the ultimate shape and quality of the work. Whiting welcomes applications for works of history, cultural or political reportage, biography, memoir, science, philosophy, criticism, graphic nonfiction, and personal essays, among other categories.

The Professional Development Opportunity Grant - For Independent Artists & Arts Organizations
https://msac.org/programs/professional-development/professional-development-opportunity-grant

This grant assists artists and arts organizations throughout Maryland in implementing best practices by embracing growth, learning, and discovery for economic sustainability. Up to $2,000 in funding will be awarded.

The FIJ Regular Grants - For Journalists

https://investigate.submittable.com/submit

This opportunity provides grants and other support to journalists for investigative stories that break new ground. This means they uncover wrongdoing in the public and private sectors and reveal information that was previously unknown or hidden. Grants are for specific investigative projects. Funding ranges from $5,000 to $10,000 to cover out-of-pocket expenses such as travel, document collection, and equipment rental. The Fund also considers requests for small stipends. The Fund provides grants for print and online articles, television and radio stories, documentaries, podcasts, and books.

Maya Angelou Book Award - For Poets

https://kclibrary.org/maba

Each year, this opportunity is given to one writer who will win $10,000, conduct a reading tour of partner colleges, universities and libraries, and be recognized in a ceremony sponsored by the Kansas City Public Library, the University of Missouri and the University of Missouri-Kansas City. In 2025, the award will be given to a work of poetry. Entries must come from publishers. Authors may not submit their works independently. Only full-length poetry collections will be considered.

The Megaphone Prize 2025 - For Poets of Color

https://radix.coop/publishing/the-megaphone-prize/

This annual contest from Radix Printing & Publishing Cooperative is dedicated to discovering timely, urgent, and interrogative collections from debut writers of color. This year, the prize is open to poetry collections by debut writers of color. One winner will receive $1,000 and 20 author copies. This opportunity seeks poetry collections that shift, exalt, renew, entangle, tear and suture, and consecrate something profound within us. They like poetry, which helps us reimagine our relationship with the written word. This prize is for manuscripts between 48 and 90 pages.

GRANTS FOR SUSTAINABILITY & GREEN BUSINESSES

The Connected Coastlines Grants

https://pulitzercenter.org/grants-fellowships/opportunities-journalists/connected-coastlines-grants

Funds journalists reporting on climate change impacts in U.S. coastal communities. Grants range from $2,000–$8,000 and prioritize science-driven storytelling.

GoodYear Community, Education, Safety Grants

https://corporate.goodyear.com/us/en/commitments/engaging-associates-and-communities/community-engagement.html

Awards up to $25,000 for projects promoting sustainability, road safety, and STEM education. Nonprofits must email community_engagement@goodyear.com to inquire.

Patagonia Corporate Grant Program

https://www.patagonia.com/how-we-fund/corporate-grant/

Provides $10,000–$20,000 to environmental nonprofits focused on conservation and activism. Priority is given to grassroots organizations with direct action campaigns.

U.S. Department of Agriculture (USDA) – Rural Business Investment Program (RBIP)

https://www.rd.usda.gov/programs-services/business-programs/rural-business-investment-program

The USDA's Rural Business Investment Program (RBIP) supports small businesses and startups in rural communities (defined as areas with populations under 50,000) by connecting them with venture capital financing. While USDA is often associated with agriculture, this program specifically targets non-farm businesses in sectors like renewable energy, technology, healthcare, and manufacturing.

GRANTS FOR TECHNOLOGY & INNOVATION

The Catalyst Fund

https://roddenberryfoundation.org/our-work/catalyst-fund/

This opportunity provides grants between $2,500 and $15,000 to anyone, anywhere in the world, with an early-stage idea or project that addresses pressing global challenges.

Emergent Ventures

https://www.mercatus.org/emergent-ventures

Funds "zero to one" innovations with scalable societal impact through grants or fellowships. Focus areas include tech, education, and healthcare.

International Game Technology's Grant Program

https://www.igt.com/en/explore-igt/about-igt/global-sustainability/supporting-our-communities/after-school-advantage-program

International Game Technology's After School Advantage Program offers up to $15,000 to schools and nonprofit organizations with the after-school program aimed to provide minority and disadvantaged children with access to state-of-the-art computer technology for learning and enhancing computer skills and meaningful use of technology resources.

Josephine Collective

https://joinjosephine.com/

Invests $10,000–$100,000 in early-stage tech startups with high-growth potential. The fund prioritizes scalable, U.S.-based ventures outside the traditional Silicon Valley ecosystem.

O'Shaughnessy Fellowships

https://www.osv.llc/oshaughnessy-fellowships

Awards $100,000 to innovators working on ambitious projects in tech, science, or social impact. Fellows receive mentorship and access to a global network of experts.

NIH COVID-19 Research Grants

https://grants.nih.gov/grants/guide/COVID-Related.cfm

Funds small businesses developing biomedical technologies to address COVID-19. Grants support research and commercialization of diagnostics, therapies, and vaccines.

NextFab Ventures | Hard-Tech Investors

https://www.f6s.com/nextfabventures/about

Invests up to $100,000 in early-stage hardware startups with patented technology. The program includes access to fabrication labs and business development support.

OpenAI Cybersecurity Grant Program

https://openai.com/blog/openai-cybersecurity-grant-program

Offers $1 million in grants to develop AI tools for cybersecurity defense. Projects must demonstrate potential to protect critical infrastructure and reduce vulnerabilities.

The Saxena Family Foundation

http://saxenafoundation.com/guidelines/

Awards up to $50,000 to U.S.-based STEM education programs and women's empowerment initiatives. Priority is given to scalable projects with measurable outcomes.

INTERNATIONAL GRANTS FOR BUSINESSES AND NONPROFITS

Her Microgrants – Amount: $500

https://aboutherculture.com/micro-grant-opportunities

Her Microgrants support Caribbean and African women entrepreneurs, creatives, and non-profit founders worldwide who are positively impacting culture and community. Recipients receive $500 to advance their projects.

Africa Innovation Mradi Research Grants – Amount: $5,000 - $10,000
https://foundation.mozilla.org/en/what-we-fund/awards/Africa-Mradi-Research-Grants/

Mozilla's Africa Innovation Mradi offers grants to individuals or organizations in Eastern and Southern Africa researching AI's impact on human rights and social justice. Six grants ranging from $5,000 to $10,000 are available.

AWS Imagine Grant - For UK and Ireland – Amount: Up to $200,000
https://aws.amazon.com/blogs/publicsector/aws-announces-expanded-imagine-grant-opportunities-for-nonprofits/

The AWS Imagine Grant provides up to $200,000 to registered nonprofits and nonprofit healthcare providers in the UK and Ireland using cloud technology to accelerate their missions. The program supports innovative projects that leverage AWS services.

Canada Digital Adoption Program – Amount: Up to $2,400
https://ised-isde.canada.ca/site/canada-digital-adoption-program/en/about-canada-digital-adoption-program

The Canada Digital Adoption Program offers grants up to $2,400 to small businesses to enhance their online presence and adopt digital technologies. The program aims to help businesses improve e-commerce and digital marketing strategies.

Cassels Small Business Grants – Amount: Up to $100,000
https://cassels.com/latest_news/cassels-launches-2024-grant-to-support-canadian-black-owned-small-business/

Cassels, supported by Wheaton Precious Metals, offers grants up to $100,000 to Black-owned or operated small businesses in Toronto, Vancouver, and Calgary. The program aims to support the growth and development of these businesses.

Citi Foundation's Global Innovation Challenge – Amount: $500,000
https://citi.fluxx.io/apply/Challenge

The Citi Foundation's Global Innovation Challenge provides catalytic grant funding to community organizations worldwide addressing homelessness. Nonprofit applicants can receive up to $500,000 to implement innovative solutions.

The Draper Richards Kaplan Foundation
https://www.drkfoundation.org/apply-for-funding/

The Draper Richards Kaplan Foundation supports social entrepreneurs with dynamic ideas that aim to create significant impact. The foundation provides funding and strategic support to early-stage organizations.

FINCA Ventures Prize – Amount: $70,000
https://fincaventures.awardsplatform.com/

The FINCA Ventures Prize awards $70,000 to social entrepreneurs committed to ending global poverty. Finalists present their pitches in Washington, D.C., focusing on innovations in environment and health sectors.

Flagship Fellowship (Watson Institute) – Amount: Up to $20,000
https://watson.is/flagship-fellowship/

The Flagship Fellowship is a 16-week program for impact-driven entrepreneurs, offering leadership training, mentorship, and a global network. Participants receive up to $20,000 to advance their ventures.

Founders Factory Africa Gen F Incubator – Amount: Up to $250,000 investment
https://www.foundersfactory.africa/gen-f-eir-initiative

Gen F supports African entrepreneurs building tech solutions to address the continent's largest challenges. The incubator offers up to $250,000 in investment and resources to scale impactful ventures.

IMPACT Grants – Amount: $1,000
https://impactfundingsolutions.com/impact-grant-application-for-businesses/

IMPACT Grants provide $1,000 to businesses and nonprofits in the U.S. and Canada making significant community contributions. The program aims to fuel endeavors that create positive social impact.

Innovate UK Grant – Amount: £75,000
https://www.nibusinessinfo.co.uk/content/women-innovation-award-202425

Innovate UK offers Women in Innovation Awards, providing £75,000 grants and tailored business support to women entrepreneurs in SMEs across the UK. The program fosters innovative ideas and business growth.

IT WORKS $5,000 Grant
https://www.ictworks.org/grants-for-african-business-entrepreneurs/

IT WORKS offers $5,000 seed funding to African entrepreneurs addressing local challenges and unlocking market opportunities. The grant supports job creation and economic growth across the continent.

Jobber Grants For Home Service Businesses – Amount: $10,000
https://getjobber.com/grants

Jobber Grants provide $10,000 to home service business owners or aspiring entrepreneurs in the U.S. and Canada (excluding Québec) to support business growth and development. The program aims to empower small businesses in the home service industry.

Launchpad for Women Entrepreneurs
https://www.launchpadforwomen.ca/

Launchpad for Women Entrepreneurs offers resources and support to early-stage women entrepreneurs across Canada. The program provides on-demand learning and in-person sessions to help women kickstart and grow successful businesses.

Lululemon Here To Be Grant – Amount: Up to $50,000
https://grants.lululemon.com/s/

Through the lululemon Community Wellbeing Grant – formerly known as Here to Be – we provide funding to community-led non-profit organizations around the globe that are advancing wellbeing through movement, mindfulness, and connection.

MEST Africa Entrepreneur Training Program
https://meltwater.org/

MEST is a Pan-African training program, seed fund, and incubator that provides aspiring technology entrepreneurs with skills in software development, business, and communications. The program offers training and funding to build successful tech companies across Africa.

The Pollination Project Micro Grants – Amount: Up to $500
https://thepollinationproject.org/

The Pollination Project offers daily micro grants of up to $500 to individuals and grassroots organizations worldwide, supporting projects that promote compassion, community, and sustainability. The grants aim to kickstart initiatives that might not qualify for traditional funding.

The Ronald W. Burkle Foundation Grant Program
http://burklefoundation.com/request-a-grant/

The Ronald W. Burkle Foundation supports programs that positively influence communities worldwide, focusing on areas such as international understanding, worker's rights, and scientific research. Interested applicants can submit a letter of inquiry through their website.

SheTrades Accelerator Programme

https://shetrades-accelerator.converve.io/

The SheTrades Accelerator Programme supports women-led businesses in the Apparel, Accessories, and Home Décor sectors from Iraq, Jordan, Kenya, Lebanon, Senegal, and South Africa. It aims to promote income generation and job creation by increasing competitiveness and creating market linkages.

Reminder: Use ChatGPT to Find More Opportunities

While this chapter provides a wide range of grant funding opportunities across industries, remember—this is just the beginning.

You can use ChatGPT to continue your search for grant funding tailored specifically to your industry, mission, and geographic location. Simply ask ChatGPT:

"Can you help me find current grant opportunities for [your business type] in [your city/state]?"

Or get even more specific:

"What grants are available in 2025 for women-owned tech startups in Atlanta, Georgia?"

Using AI tools like ChatGPT allows you to find real-time, updated information that aligns with your unique goals. Make it a habit to check in weekly, it's a smart, time-saving way to stay ahead and stay funded!

IN CONCLUSION

You did it! You made it through *The Money Resource Guide: Grants, Business Capital & Smart Money Strategies for Sustainable Growth.* That speaks volumes about your commitment to growing your business or nonprofit with purpose, strategy, and power. You're no longer in the dark, you're equipped with the knowledge, tools, and resources to confidently pursue and secure the funding you deserve.

I want you to remember this: Grant Funding is not a one-time event, it's a consistent strategy. Just like you show up for your business every day, you must also show up for your funding journey. The most successful entrepreneurs and organizations are the ones who apply *consistently.* Every "no" gets you one step closer to a life-changing "yes."

So stay in action. Keep showing up. Keep believing. And keep applying. You're not on this journey alone, I'm here cheering you on every step of the way. When you win (and *you will*), I want to know about it so we can celebrate your success together!

Share Your Wins: Your success matters. It inspires others, and it shows what's possible when preparation meets opportunity. Your win could be the spark that lights someone else's path.

Take 2 minutes to fill out the Grant Funding Win Form:
https://bit.ly/2024ShareYourWins
Let's celebrate you and shout your win from the rooftops!

To your continued growth and prosperity,
– Renee Bobb

TRACKING YOUR WORK

TRACKING FORM

GRANT FUNDING ACTIVITY TRACKER

As you begin applying for grants and connecting with potential funders, it's essential to stay organized and track your outreach efforts. Keeping a detailed record of every grant opportunity you pursue, including contact information, submission dates, and outcomes, will help you stay focused, follow up effectively, and avoid missing deadlines or duplicating efforts.

Use the form below to document each grant you apply for. This system will not only keep you organized but will also give you a clear picture of your progress and patterns over time as you build a sustainable funding strategy.

SAMPLE ENTRY

Grant Name	The Michael & Susan Dell Foundation
Website	https://www.dell.org
Due Date	Ongoing
Special Requirements	None
Date of Submission	March 21, 2025
Results	Waiting for Response
Grant Announcement Date	June 3, 2025

YOUR TRACKER

Grant Name	
Website	
Due Date	
Special Requirements	
Date of Submission	
Results	
Grant Announcement Date	

YOUR TRACKER

Grant Name	
Website	
Due Date	
Special Requirements	
Date of Submission	
Results	
Grant Announcement Date	

YOUR TRACKER

Grant Name	
Website	
Due Date	
Special Requirements	
Date of Submission	
Results	
Grant Announcement Date	

YOUR TRACKER

Grant Name	
Website	
Due Date	
Special Requirements	
Date of Submission	
Results	
Grant Announcement Date	

YOUR TRACKER

Grant Name	
Website	
Due Date	
Special Requirements	
Date of Submission	
Results	
Grant Announcement Date	

YOUR TRACKER

Grant Name	
Website	
Due Date	
Special Requirements	
Date of Submission	
Results	
Grant Announcement Date	

YOUR TRACKER

Grant Name	
Website	
Due Date	
Special Requirements	
Date of Submission	
Results	
Grant Announcement Date	

YOUR TRACKER

Grant Name	
Website	
Due Date	
Special Requirements	
Date of Submission	
Results	
Grant Announcement Date	

YOUR TRACKER

Grant Name	
Website	
Due Date	
Special Requirements	
Date of Submission	
Results	
Grant Announcement Date	

YOUR TRACKER

Grant Name	
Website	
Due Date	
Special Requirements	
Date of Submission	
Results	
Grant Announcement Date	

YOUR TRACKER

Grant Name	
Website	
Due Date	
Special Requirements	
Date of Submission	
Results	
Grant Announcement Date	

YOUR TRACKER

Grant Name	
Website	
Due Date	
Special Requirements	
Date of Submission	
Results	
Grant Announcement Date	

YOUR TRACKER

Grant Name	
Website	
Due Date	
Special Requirements	
Date of Submission	
Results	
Grant Announcement Date	

YOUR TRACKER

Grant Name	
Website	
Due Date	
Special Requirements	
Date of Submission	
Results	
Grant Announcement Date	

YOUR TRACKER

Grant Name	
Website	
Due Date	
Special Requirements	
Date of Submission	
Results	
Grant Announcement Date	

YOUR TRACKER

Grant Name	
Website	
Due Date	
Special Requirements	
Date of Submission	
Results	
Grant Announcement Date	

YOUR TRACKER

Grant Name	
Website	
Due Date	
Special Requirements	
Date of Submission	
Results	
Grant Announcement Date	

YOUR TRACKER

Grant Name	
Website	
Due Date	
Special Requirements	
Date of Submission	
Results	
Grant Announcement Date	

YOUR TRACKER

Grant Name	
Website	
Due Date	
Special Requirements	
Date of Submission	
Results	
Grant Announcement Date	

YOUR TRACKER

Grant Name	
Website	
Due Date	
Special Requirements	
Date of Submission	
Results	
Grant Announcement Date	

YOUR TRACKER

Grant Name	
Website	
Due Date	
Special Requirements	
Date of Submission	
Results	
Grant Announcement Date	

YOUR TRACKER

Grant Name	
Website	
Due Date	
Special Requirements	
Date of Submission	
Results	
Grant Announcement Date	

YOUR TRACKER

Grant Name	
Website	
Due Date	
Special Requirements	
Date of Submission	
Results	
Grant Announcement Date	

YOUR TRACKER

Grant Name	
Website	
Due Date	
Special Requirements	
Date of Submission	
Results	
Grant Announcement Date	

YOUR TRACKER

Grant Name	
Website	
Due Date	
Special Requirements	
Date of Submission	
Results	
Grant Announcement Date	

YOUR TRACKER

Grant Name	
Website	
Due Date	
Special Requirements	
Date of Submission	
Results	
Grant Announcement Date	

YOUR TRACKER

Grant Name	
Website	
Due Date	
Special Requirements	
Date of Submission	
Results	
Grant Announcement Date	

YOUR TRACKER

Grant Name	
Website	
Due Date	
Special Requirements	
Date of Submission	
Results	
Grant Announcement Date	

YOUR TRACKER

Grant Name	
Website	
Due Date	
Special Requirements	
Date of Submission	
Results	
Grant Announcement Date	

YOUR TRACKER

Grant Name	
Website	
Due Date	
Special Requirements	
Date of Submission	
Results	
Grant Announcement Date	

ABOUT BUSINESS COACH RENEE BOBB

Philanthropist • Bestselling Author • AI & Grant
Funding Strategist • Empowerment Trainer

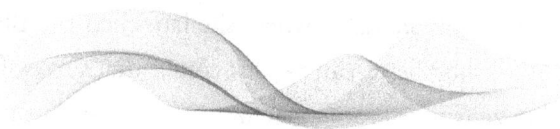

Renee Bobb is a nationally recognized business coach, award-winning entrepreneur, and bestselling author with over 20 years of experience empowering small businesses, nonprofit organizations, and startups to thrive. As the CEO of Renee Bobb Training, LLC (www.ReneeBobbTraining.com), Renee leads a powerhouse Empowerment Training and Development Firm specializing in AI for Business and Nonprofits, Grant Funding Strategy, Revenue Diversification, and Financial Empowerment.

A passionate advocate for equity, education, and economic empowerment, Renee currently serves as a Business Coach with Hello Alice and the Comcast RISE Grant Program, where she has coached over 120 business owners who received Comcast RISE funding helping them build sustainable businesses through strategic growth, financial planning, and the integration of AI technology.

Renee is also a Nonprofit Capacity Building Consultant working with nationally respected organizations like United Way, Pathway Women's Business Center and Safe Haven Family Shelter. Through her workshops and coaching, she teaches nonprofit agencies how to secure multi-year grant funding, integrate productivity tools, and create long-term sustainability.

As Founder of the Grant Funding Academy (https://www.skool.com/thegrantfundingacademy), Renee has helped her clients secure over $2.3 million in grant funding. She is widely known for her ability to simplify the grant funding process and equip entrepreneurs with tools to win funding and scale their businesses. She is also a trailblazer in delivering AI Integration and Business Automation Training, helping small businesses streamline operations and increase productivity.

Renee's past leadership includes serving as the Director of Training & Development at Bunker Labs, where she launched the Black Veteran Entrepreneur Workshop Series, an 8-week course that successfully trained and supported dozens of minority veteran-owned businesses. This initiative has since expanded nationally to serve Latinx, Asian American, and female Veterans and military families.

A decorated U.S. Navy Veteran, Renee served as a Telecommunications Operator with Top Secret Clearance. She is the owner of the Music City Icons Professional Women's Basketball Team (https://www.musiccityicons.com/) a platform that helps women reignite their basketball careers and serves as a pipeline to the WNBA and international teams.

Renee is also a prolific author, having published over 20 books including:

- *The Self-Publishing Process: The Beginner's Guide to Book Publishing Success*
- *Financial Empowerment: A Practical Approach to Getting Your Financial Life in Order*
- *Thrive in 2025: Financial Empowerment Planner*

Her work has been recognized nationally, earning prestigious awards such as:

- Mighty 25 Military Influencer Award
- Dr. Paris Love Military/Entrepreneur Award

- Tennessee Christian Chamber of Commerce Community Impact Award
- Nashville Business Journal Veteran of the Year
- SBA Women in Business Champion of the Year

Renee holds a B.S. in Interdisciplinary Studies from Norfolk State University and is a proud member of Zeta Phi Beta Sorority, Incorporated.

The Money Resource Guide: Grants, Business Capital & Smart Money Strategies for Sustainable Growth
Fourth Edition

Empowerment Training & Development Coaching Firm

Renee Bobb, Empowerment Coach

(615) 753-5647
bobbrenee@yahoo.com
www.ReneeBobbTraining.com
https://stan.store/reneebobbtraining
https://www.skool.com/thegrantfundingacademy

To order additional copies of
The Money Resource Guide: Grants, Business Capital & Smart Money Strategies for Sustainable Growth
Fourth Edition

Renee is available for one-on-one business coaching and consultations. As well as speaking engagements, seminars and workshops.